PERFECT ANSWERS TO INTERVIEW QUESTIONS

All you need to get it right first time

Max Eggert

Published by Random House Business Books in 2005

Copyright © Max Eggert 2005

First published in the UK by Random House Business Books in 2005

Random House Business Books
20 Vauxhall Bridge Road
London SW1V 2SA

Random House Australia (Pty) Limited
20 Alfred Street, Milsons Point
Sydney, New South Wales 2061, Australia

Random House New Zealand Limited
18 Poland Road, Glenfield
Auckland 10, New Zealand

Random House South Africa (Pty) Limited
Endulini, 5a Jubilee Road, Parktown 2193, South Africa

The Random House Group Limited Reg. No. 954009

Papers used by Random House are natural, recyclable
products made from wood grown in sustainable forests. The
manufacturing processes conform to the environmental regulations
of the country of origin.

ISBN 1 8441 3461 0

Companies, institutions and other organisations wishing to make
bulk purchases of any business books published by Random House
should contact their local bookstore or Random House direct:
Special Sales Director
Random House, 20 Vauxhall Bridge Road, London SW1V 2SA

Tel: 020 7840 8470 Fax: 020 7828 6681

www.randomhouse.co.uk
businessbooks@randomhouse.co.uk

Typeset in Sabon by SX Composing DTP, Rayleigh, Essex
Printed and bound in Great Britain by
Bookmarque Ltd, Croydon, Surrey

Contents

Preface

This book is born out of the scar tissue of the hundreds of individuals I have interviewed and the thousands I have coached through interviews first as an HR professional and then as a management psychologist specializing in the areas of Career Development and Outplacement.

Perfect is a big call since each interviewer and interviewee brings so many variables to the selection process. The only rule that we have about interviews is that there are no rules but there are principles and it is those principles that I have attempted to capture and share with you in this little book.

If I could guarantee – and consultants in anything never give guarantees – that you would get the job offer if you followed everything suggested in the following pages then the fee for this book would be far higher. However, the assurance that I can give you is that if you use the advice and suggestions given here you will be able to present yourself much better and really increase your chances of a job offer.

It is unfair and unjust that:

It is not the best person that gets the job but the one that is best on the day of the interview

so our purpose is to help you become the best you can be in what is always a competitive field.

At Transcareer we never wish people good luck in their interviews but wish them well in their preparation for therein lies the foundation of their career success.

Max A. Eggert
Bondi Beach
Australia

Dedication:
To Michelle and Kirrili who, as my interns, did most of the psychological research for this project. Thanks to you both for making it such fun and for teaching me what I should already know. Love to you both.

Introduction

The purpose of this little book is to get you 'interview fit'. Every interviewer is different and has their own set of favourite questions that they like to ask their candidates. Not only this but also interview questions are like clothes for teenagers in that they go through fashions very quickly. All this means is that it would be impossible to predict the exact topics that might get covered in your interview but here you should find the majority of the types of questions that you are likely to get asked.

The questioning process during an interview usually follows this standard structure:

Rapport questions — to settle you down and for the interviewer to show that he or she is human and not a Gestapo interrogator. The more relaxed you are the more likely you are to reveal your true self.

Experience questions — beginning with your most recent working history and working back in time picking up on the strengths of your experience and testing the gaps.

Technical questions – these questions are about specific skills required in the position and whether or not you possess them. The bulk of the time is usually spent here.

Challenge questions – it is unlikely that these questions will come early unless it becomes obvious that you have incorrectly been shortlisted. There is no such thing as the perfect candidate; everyone will be lacking in some or other skill, competency or experience. The interviewer might challenge you on the areas where you might be an employment risk because of your lack of experience or qualifications. Nor should you be concerned if you are challenged – you would not be interviewed if the interviewer thought that you could not do the job.

Invitation questions – the opportunity for you to ask any questions you may have.

This book will guide you through all these types of questions showing you why they are asked and, where appropriate, providing suggested answers. Technical questions pose a difficulty for a book like this because it would be impossible to cover the thousands of jobs that exist today.

Interviews are both easy and difficult at the same time. Easy because you are going to be talking about yourself and you know more about yourself than anyone else and certainly a lot more than the interviewer. Difficult because depending on what you say and how you say it you will either secure the job or have to keep looking for another.

Unless you are a real job hopper it is unlikely that you will have more than ten interviews during the whole of your career. Now anything that you do only ten times over a time span of at least 40 years is unlikely to become a real skill. Car salesmen negotiate deals every day of their working life so even if you buy a car every year, who, on a skills alone basis, is likely to get the better deal? Interviewers, similarly, have far more experience and skill than you so unless you are fully prepared you are going to be at a significant disadvantage. Here we are going to redress the balance for you.

All is not lost or as difficult as you might think. One of the best things about an interview, as we said about Challenge questions, is that you are only seen by a recruiter if he or she thinks that you have a pretty good chance of getting the job in the first place. Why would they want to see a 'no hoper'. Once you have secured the interview the interviewer has already decided that you have the necessary skills and experience to do the job successfully. What is interesting about the selection process is that at the CV stage recruiters are looking for reasons to turn you down because they have so many applicants and only want a short list of five or so. Once you get to the interview the mindset of the interviewer does an about-face and for each candidate they ask themselves 'Can I take this person on?'

Another thing in your favour is that whilst interviewers may have lots of experience very few of them have had any formal training in how to interview professionally. A recent survey suggested that as few as 15% of managers have had any formal training in interviewing skills. This means that once you have read this book and worked through the activities, you have an 85% chance of knowing more about interviewing than the person asking the questions – that is a real plus for you.

Your situation gets even better since the higher up in the management food chain your interviewer is the less likely he or she is to have had training! Strange, senior executives ensure that their junior staff are trained in interviewing skills but they do not think selection skills are necessary for themselves. Just think, once you have read this book you will know more about interviewing than most interviewers. Now that is a real advantage!

Interviews are funny things really. Rather like a first date both parties are on their very best behaviour: the interviewer presenting the best picture of the employer, and you, the interviewee, presenting the best picture of yourself as possible. Because 'best' first impressions are given and received on both sides of the interview table it is no wonder that so many employment relationships end up in a divorce down the employment track.

I suppose, really, the best things about the interview are that:

a) it is not astrophysics to learn the basics and work out what sort of questions you are likely to be asked.

b) you are, of course, in total control of every word that comes out of your mouth.

When you follow only some of the advice, ideas and concepts in this book you will be in control of what you say, know what information you wish to disclose and how it should be delivered. And all this information will certainly make you a powerful candidate.

It would be wise to follow the maxim below while you prepare for your interview:

If it is going to be, it is down to me

Only you can be at the interview and it will be up to you to convince the interviewer(s) of your talents – remember they don't have a crystal ball. And, as unfair as it may seem, just like creating a first impression, you only get one shot.

Whilst we cannot guarantee that we will get you the job offer – that always goes to the best candidate but we can promise, providing you work hard at your preparation, that you will be able to give your best at any interview and not come out of an interview saying 'If only I'd . . .' or 'Next time I'll say . . .'

Why candidates fail at interviews

THE TEN ALMOST DEADLY SINS

1. They are not prepared
Essentially the interview process is a selling activity and you, the interviewee, are the product. If you do not know the product inside out and back to front you will not be able to secure the job. If the salesman cannot answer the questions on the topics that the buyer needs to know about, then a sale, that is the job offer, is most unlikely.

We have some strategies for you – see page 30.

2. They do not think through what the interviewer wants
The interviewer has a problem: there are things in the organisation that need to be done and currently are not happening because of a staff shortage. By the time the vacancy has landed on the HR recruiter's desk the requirements are pretty well nailed down in terms of specifics about what is required and the sort of person best suited to the position. These requirements usually form and underpin the structure and language of the job

advert. So many applicants work really hard on their preliminary paper work and CV to get to the selection stage and then subsequently fail to prepare for the interview with the same amount of diligence and effort.

We have some strategies for you – see page 39.

3. They concentrate on what they want out of a job/employer rather than on what they have to offer

Of course you want the job for the money, the status and what it is going to do for your future career prospects but if you approach the interview from this perspective you will surely fail. No shopkeeper puts a big sign in capital letters and flashing neon lights outside their shop saying: 'Come in because we want to make a profit out of you'. No, they present the wares, goods and services in the best possible way they can hoping that you will choose them and what they are offering rather than taking your custom somewhere else.

We have some strategies for you – see page 48.

4. They do not know what it is they are presenting (selling) to the employer

This relates to not knowing yourself as a product. Even if the job titles happen to be identical, no two jobs in different organisations are ever the same. It does not matter if you are an accountant or road sweeper, a research chemist or if you work in the mailroom, positions are always organisation specific with their own peculiarities and special needs. Like fighting a war, the better your intelligence, the better your chance of winning.

We have some strategies for you – see page 30.

5. They cannot express themselves fluently

Interviews are unfair to half the world of people that we

label as introverts. Extroverts during interviews get a good deal because they 'talk – think – talk' whereas introverts 'think – talk – think'. The implication here is that introverts, if we can stereotype them, tend to be slower of speech because they much prefer to provide considered answers. The difficulty is that most interviewers want the information quickly so that they can move onto the next candidate. Unfortunately for the slow speakers amongst us the research suggests that people who are really fluent are rated by the ordinary person as being more intelligent, with better interpersonal skills and make better managers. This is obviously nonsense and untrue but we are dealing with perceptions here. Then there is the problem of the 'tip of the tongue' phenomena.

We have some strategies for you – see page 68.

6. They lack rapport skills
Interviewers are human and they will recruit people that they like and with whom they can get on. After all, they are going to have to work with you. Why would you take on people that you thought were geeks or you did not like? If you demonstrate rapport skills during and after the interview then this will go a long way to smoothing the relationship between yourself and the interviewer and make you a more attractive candidate.

We have some strategies for you – see page 163.

7. They suffer from anxiety
Unfortunately interviews are like exams and, as unfair as it is, it is how you perform on the day that counts. Replays and second takes do not occur in interviews. Selection would be great, and much fairer, if it were like continuous assessment at school, then your true worth could be demonstrated, but the interview is a one-shot

affair. If you suffer from nerves that interfere with your memory, your thinking ability, your ability to speak fluently or your rapport skills then you must do something about this to secure the position you want.

We have some strategies for you – see pages 16 and 146.

8. They 'white elephant' themselves

You white elephant yourself when you volunteer negative information about yourself when it was not requested by the interviewer. Before the interview you keep reminding yourself that you must not tell the interviewer about your white elephant (for example, that you are not well qualified) then in the middle of the interview you say something like 'Although I don't have an MBA . . .' and you have just gift wrapped and delivered your white elephant.

We have some strategies for you – see page 78.

How to win the PTD (Polite Turn Down) you don't want

BEING LATE FOR THE INTERVIEW OR APPEARING UNRELIABLE

Interviews are scheduled one after the other so you can imagine what happens when you are late – it throws the whole day out. In fact it doesn't: you get a short interview and you don't get the job. Interview behaviour is projected and interpreted as work behaviour. If you can't organise yourself to get to the interview on time what is your commitment to the work likely to be?

BEING ARROGANT

Not many people are arrogant at interviews but some use arrogance to hide their anxiety or they think it cool to appear as if they are not that interested in the job and the firm will be lucky to get them. With such behaviour you will be very lucky if you get the job offer.

NOT TELLING THE TRUTH

A cardinal sin. Even if they give you the job it is grounds for dismissal. Let them hire the true you not some fantasy that you have of yourself. I don't know anyone who has not put a gloss on their performance when going for a job they wanted but there is a definite line between a gloss and telling lies; don't cross it.

TRYING TO BE FUNNY

Selection is a serious business. Recruiters put their jobs on the line every time they recommend someone to a senior line manager. You might think that some light relief might be welcome in the hard day's work of a selector by injecting some humour. Yes, you will be remembered but not so you get hired.

APPEARING IRRESPONSIBLE

Of course you are not going to 'fess up to being irresponsible but your past might let you down – not using a gap year wisely, moving in and out of jobs quickly without adequate explanations, and yes, you do appear irresponsible when you do not take the interview seriously as a coping mechanism for your interview nerves.

Also watch being passionate when disclosing your enthusiasm for bungee jumping, leaping out of perfectly good aircraft or abseiling off tall buildings unless, of course, you are applying for a position with the SAS.

LACKING MANNERS

You should treat your interviewer and the support staff with respect. Quite frequently I have had someone be charming to me only to discover later that they have been perfectly obnoxious to my staff. Frequently a manager will ask his or her secretary: 'Well, what do you think?'

LACKING IN MOTIVATION

You have to appear as if you want the job for its own sake and not just as an income stream. If you attend the interview because 'the dole office sent you', then mention this right away and both parties can play the game. It is hard enough for managers to motivate staff anyway so a little motivation at the start is most welcome.

BEING EXTREME

Interviewers are risk adverse. If you are extreme in any area alarm bells will start ringing and you will be struck off the short list. Be average except where you can shine in terms of skills and interests.

COMPLAINING OR BLAMING

You have to be like the good salesman who never knocks the competition, but just concentrates on how good the product is. You must be positive about previous bosses and previous employers irrespective of how badly you have been treated. Most streets are two-way and you don't want the interviewer thinking about your possible contribution to a difficult situation.

BEING TOTALLY SELF-CENTRED

Of course you want the job for your own reasons and you know what you want to do, but if you appear self-centred during the interview this might conflict with what your future employer wants you to do.

THE EARLY BIRD CATCHES THE JOB

Before we even start on the questions we have to get this across first. You could know all the perfect answers but if you are late for the interview you will not be able to use them. It is essential that you arrive early for the interview. How early? 20–30 minutes early. Here's why:

Murphy's Law could apply to your travel arrangements, finding the office, the weather, industrial action on public transport, etc. Being early gives a time buffer in which you can afford to be late, get lost, dry out or find an alternative form of transport.

In an attempt to be fair, selectors set the same allocation of time for each candidate. If you are 30 minutes late do not expect an extension on your interview time. Like an exam, the finish time is still the same if you arrive late. You know that you were late because of reasons beyond your control but your interviewer will put it down to a lack of motivation, planning, self-management and a whole host of other negatives. Also, if he or she is seeing six other candidates on that day – all of whom look from their CVs like they can do the job – why should they put the whole schedule out because of you? So arrive early.

At any interview there is an understandable amount of anxiety. This is good because the adrenalin will help you perform but as you know from other stressful activities too much anxiety can actually harm performance.

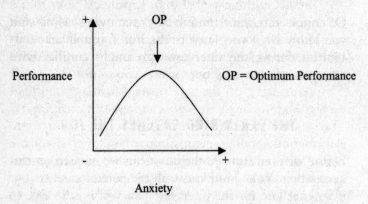

Now the body will naturally calm itself down with time as you acclimatise to the interview environment. So whilst you are at your prospective employer's offices your anxiety levels will look like this:

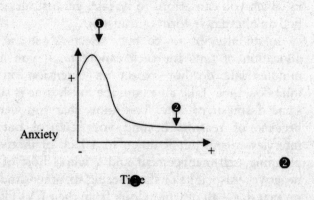

It is obvious that being interviewed at position   is far better than at position 1. Who can do their best at interviews when their tummy has butterflies, is rumbling, they have sweaty palms and feet (one of which just won't stop tapping up and down)? I exaggerate but you know what I mean.

There is nothing worse than getting an hour into a two-hour interview and being reminded somewhat insistently by your bladder that it is full and demands immediate relief. Anxiety also increases this need. Arrive early and use the facilities.

Interestingly, on the way to the facilities you might be fortunate enough to pass a company notice board. This should be read thoroughly to give you extra information about your prospective employer. If you are really fortunate the 'internal vacancies section' might even have details of the job you are going for.

So arrive early

Formal interview structures

Interviews are obviously not casual conversations since both you and the interviewer have objectives: you want to be offered the position; the interviewer wants to see if you are the best fit. Interviewers need to get the information they require to make an appropriate decision and to assist them in this task various systems or interview structures have been developed.

We cover this here because if you, the interviewee, understand and can recognise the structure or process that the interviewer is using, you can anticipate the questions or at least understand where the interviewer is coming from and the reason for the questions. In much the same way a good batsman will know what sort of ball he is being bowled and anticipate an appropriate stroke well before the ball leaves the hand of the bowler.

Knowing the possible structures also provides an advantage in helping you prepare for the interview because you can anticipate the questions that you might get asked in each of the various categories.

THE SEVEN-POINT PLAN

This is perhaps the grandfather of all the interview structures – well over 50 years old now – but it is still in use because it is so comprehensive and many organisations use it to develop the person specification (which is the profile that has been constructed for the 'ideal candidate').

Let's deal with the seven points one by one.

1. Physical attributes
Your physical attributes are important for some jobs. Salespeople are expected to be clean and presentable, senior managers are expected to have gravitas, security people need to look fit. Sometimes a physical attribute is necessary because of the job requirements. Firemen, for instance, need a certain chest size and inhalation expansion ability for obvious reasons, policemen need to be able to run and aspiring pilots will fail if they are colour blind.

You can't do a great deal about much of your physical attributes but you can think through what the ideal person for the job would look like in terms of dress and style and how they might carry themselves. Fortunately interviewers are not able to discriminate on gender and, not before time, soon they will not be able to discriminate on age. On the latter you can help yourself by looking critically at your interview wardrobe, get fit and revamp your accessories – yes, shoes, watches, pens, glasses, hairstyles and even make-up styles are all the victims of fashion. Giving yourself an interview makeover is really worth the investment.

These points are more fully addressed in the sister book to this *Perfect Interview*.

2. Attainments

This comes in two parts, namely: your academic attainments and those of your career.

If you are under 30 you might do well to anticipate some questions on your academic development. For example:

- Why did you choose that topic?
- How has your degree assisted you in your career?
- Why is your career path different to your course of study?

But once you are over 30, unless you have just taken or are doing something such as an MBA as a mature student, all the questions will be directed to your attainments at work. Questions that the interviewer will be asking will be around the competencies required by the job, the skills and experience that you have brought to the table and what caused the major shifts in your employment pattern. We deal with all these aspects later. You might also get some questions to discover your management style, your preferred team role, your motivation and interpersonal skills. Again, we deal with these later.

3. General intelligence

Sensible selectors will be assessing your IQ – we might think of IQ as your innate problem-solving ability or your brainpower. Not only do they want someone who is bright enough for the job but also someone who is not too bright. Recruiters know that if they take on someone too bright they are either going to get bored very quickly and leave, or stay and become a difficult employee unless they can be promoted to a level more suited to their brainpower.

Some people, especially those who have been retrenched, go for jobs below their capability. They are surprised and go through masses of self-doubt when they get turned down for jobs they could do standing on their head. More than likely they were rejected not because they could not do the job but because they had too many smarts for the job on offer. I am not suggesting here that you should 'dumb down' in order to get a job but rather go for positions that match your IQ, then both you and the employer will benefit.

Some firms give ability tests but a professional interviewer can usually tell how bright someone is and can correctly place them in one of five categories: brilliant, clever, average, below average and, finally, intellectually challenged. For most jobs this simple categorisation more than suffices.

4. How to appear smarter than you are

Here are six tips on how to impress your interviewer with your intellectual prowess:

- Speak fluently – this is not to say that those of us who are slow of speech are also slow mentally but it is rare to find someone who is very fluent but not bright as well.
- Use long words – size of vocabulary is an indication of intelligence – the more words you use with more than two syllables the brighter you are supposed to be. (However, do not lose your interviewer!)
- Juggle concepts – if you can keep four or five concepts going at the same time in your conversation then you are probably very clever because most of us can only manage two or three.
- Generate alternatives quickly – usually a creative brain is a clever brain.

- See the implications of your decisions – sometimes called 'the helicopter view'. Being able to rise above the requirements of the day and see both the context and implications of what you are doing is one of the signs of a high IQ.
- Have a vision – this is similar to the previous item but it is to have a long-term view of where you are going and what you want to achieve. Most of us live in a three-month window – just seeing what we did three months ago and what we need to do in the next three months. By enjoying a longer perspective you are being strategic and strategists are the clever people amongst us.

However, do not try and outsmart your interviewer. Intellectual arrogance never won a job.

As I have said most interviewers can place you on their rough and ready IQ scale but there is one question from a professional interviewer which, if you get it, you know is the IQ question.

Most interviewers are trained to ask simple questions one at a time but the exception is the IQ question:

What have been the major changes in your work over the past five years, how have they impacted on your work and what do you think will be the changes that we can look forward to in the next five years?

Here you have three conceptual questions all bowled down to you at once! Here is the key:

Average intelligence – you answer just one of the questions

Clever	– you answer two of the questions
Brilliant	– you answer all three questions

This relates back to the point about being able to hold multiple concepts in your head.

So if you want to appear brilliant, and the job calls for it, when you get asked the multiple 'conceptual' question my advice would be to repeat the question out loud before you answer it and as you answer each section move your thumb from your index finger to your second finger to your ring finger as an aide-mémoire – keeping your hand out of sight of the interviewer of course!

5. Special abilities

Some of us might not be as clever as others but we do have exceptional gifts in one or two areas. Savants are an extreme example of this in their mathematical and calendar ability. You might not have a degree in engineering or even be able to write an essay but you might be able to tell what is wrong with a car engine by listening to it and be able to strip the engine down to correct the fault. Some people have number ability, some are good with space and three-dimensional manipulation, some have an exceptional ability to remember facts. People have all sorts of gifts, and for some jobs where special abilities are required, recruiters are going to be very interested to see if you possess them.

6. Interests

Now it usually surprises people when they get one of the following questions:

• **What do you do in your spare time?**

23

- **What are your interests outside work?**

because they feel that what they do in their free time is their own business. What they forget is this: what we do with our spare money and our spare time – the two disposables that are within our total control – can tell someone a lot about our values, interests, motivations and the sort of person we really are. There is likely to be a real difference between someone who collects stamps and breeds tropical fish and someone who is a member of Rotary and looks after a Scout troop. Irrespective of their skills and competencies one is more likely to be better working in data management and the other on a telephone helpline. Sweeping generalisations are dangerous but there is no smoke without fire.

See page 21 for ways to tackle the Interest questions.

7. Disposition
Disposition is just a fancy name for personality but without all the emotive concepts that are associated with the word. As hinted in the Interests section above, certain personality types are naturally more suited to certain jobs or professions.

Stereotypically, salespeople are supposed to be extroverted and outgoing. HR people are thought to be helpful and service-orientated. Again generalities about people's personalities can be both helpful and dangerous.

Freud suggested that 'the child is the father of the man' so please do not attempt to change your personality, but rather be aware that how you come across in terms of your disposition will have a direct bearing on the interviewer's decision.

CIRCUMSTANCES

Certain jobs require a potential job holder to have circumstances which will support the position. Shift-workers need to be able to work shifts. It is acceptable to expect employees to live within a reasonable commuting distance of their work. Catholic priests are expected to be heterosexual yet celibate. Not too long ago, it was thought helpful for senior executives to have a 'corporate wife' to support them and project the right image. It is interesting to observe that we usually see politicians' partners at election time and then they tend to disappear once their other half gets into office.

Most interviewers will stay away from this area because of the plethora of equality legislation, but you would do well, in preparing for the interview, to think through the question: 'How do my circumstances help or hinder my application?' Perhaps, more importantly, you should ask yourself the question: 'Will this job support or be detrimental to the lifestyle that I and my family want?'

TARGETED INTERVIEWING

At the time of writing, this is fast becoming the most popular form of interviewing. It concentrates on actual experience based on the premise that the best indicator of future performance is past performance. This form of selection is most common in the Public Sector and the larger firms that have the HR departments which can undertake the depth of analysis required, to identify the competencies required by the job and afford the training of their interviewers in the process.

This form of interviewing is a very powerful tool in

PERFECT ANSWERS TO INTERVIEW QUESTIONS

the interviewer's armoury because it is very difficult for candidates to fudge their answers even if they have the gift of the gab, and have kissed the blarney stone several times.

In targeted interviewing a great deal of effort goes into examining the target position and teasing out the competencies required to be able to do the job effectively. These become the selection criteria for the position.

You know when your interviewer is using this system through the structure of the questions. For example;

- Tell me about a time when . . .
- Give me a specific example of . . .
- What have your specifically done in the area of . . .

All the questions are structured so that you cannot waffle or give hypothetical answers.

The structure of questions during the interview

Most interviews follow a basic interviewing structure. Unless you get a very perverse interviewer, and they do exist, it is unlikely that you will get the hard questions or the challenges as soon as the interview begins. However, because the selector has to make absolutely sure you are the right person for the job, the interview is not just going to be a social chat.

So that you can relax and give your best, most interviews have an easy–hard–easy structure:

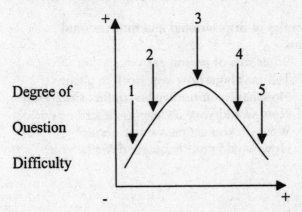

Passage of time during the interview

1. Examples of social questions and statements

    i.   Good to see you and thanks for coming on time.

    ii.   How are you today?

    iii.   Was it easy to park?

    iv.   Was the motorway busy?

2. Examples of opening questions based on your CV

    i.   Tell me about yourself.

    ii.   What have you been doing recently?

    iii.   What did you like about that job?

    iv.   Why did you stay so long with the company?

    v.   Why did you leave?

3. Examples of testing questions

    i.   Tell me about a time when you . . .

    ii.   What have you found difficult in your job?

    iii.   Who do you find it challenging to work with?

    iv.   What stresses you at work; give me an example.

    v.   What are your weaknesses?

    vi.   Why were you made redundant?

    vii.   Why have you been out of work so long?

4. Examples of dispositional and motivational questions

    i.   What sort of person are you?

    ii.   Tell me about how you work in a team.

    iii.   How have you resolved a conflict situation?

    iv.   How would your colleagues describe you?

    v.   What do you get passionate about?

    vi.   How would your manager describe you?

5. Examples of closing questions and statements

i. Where else have you applied?
ii. What training do you think you might need?
iii. Have you any questions for us?
iv. The next stage is . . .
v. We'll get back to you by . . .
vi. What's next for you today?
vii. Thank you for coming.

Preparation for questions

As we have already discovered, being interviewed is essentially a selling process where you are both the product and the salesperson. The interviewer is the buyer. Many feel that they are no good at selling themselves but it really is not that difficult mainly because we have already established that the interviewer is very interested in you, otherwise you would not be seen. So rather than trying to give the hard sell, all you are doing is attempting to present yourself in the best possible light. Always remember you are an applicant and not a supplicant. Think of the interview as a career discussion, a mutual exploration of what each party has to offer the other.

Now you can only present yourself once you know yourself. Again you have the advantage because you know yourself and your career history better than anyone else. However, you must do some work on yourself and your career history. Most of us can remember what we have done in the last year but it could be that what you did five years ago is appropriate to the job you are going for.

Following are some activities for you:

List your achievements
List at least five achievements from every job you have had going right back to the beginning of your working life. Most of us find it easy to remember what we have achieved recently but interviewers will want to review the majority of your career because the best indicator of future performance is past performance.

Some interviewers will even want to start right at the beginning, from your first job and work through your career; more sensible interviewers will start with your present position and work backwards in time. You will get the odd interviewer who feels they have to be in control, and to prove how much he or she knows; they will comb your CV to find something they know about and will begin their questioning there. Since you cannot predict what type of interviewer you will have it is a good idea to review the whole of your career in terms of your achievements.

FABing

In thinking about your achievements it is important to do three things which we call FABing – that is, divide your achievements into three parts:

Feature	– What you actually did/do in your job.
Analysis	– How big was it in terms of monetary value, numbers or a percentage?
Benefit	– What did your employer gain from what you did?

For stacks more information on how you can do this please see the sister book to this entitled *Perfect CV*.

Your job description is a good place to start. For example, it might have:

- To produce monthly reports
- To do the cash banking

If you FAB these job requirements they might look like:

- Produced monthly cash-flow reports for management and never missed a due date in three years
- Banked up to £8,000 in any one day to ensure maximum cash flow and overnight security

The fact that you usually banked £2000 and this was a special day during the sales is neither here nor there because you actually did it.

THEME YOUR ACHIEVEMENTS

Once you have completed your achievement list, see what themes emerge, for example: leadership, communication, creativity, motivation, strategy, etc. This will help you answer questions such as:

- **Tell me about your leadership style.**
- **What are your strengths?**

because the supplementary question is going to be: 'Can you give me an example?' Having prepared your achievement list you will have no difficulty in delivering a brilliant illustration which is quantified and which shows how you added value to your employer – the implication is of course that you can do the same for your prospective employer.

UNIQUE SELLING POINTS

What are your trump cards?
Your interviewer has a real problem. 'To which of the short-listed candidates should I make an offer?' It is your responsibility to make sure that during the interview you have presented those aspects of your background that give you the best chance of being that person, the ideal candidate. In other words, what makes you special? These are known as your USPs – your Unique Selling Points.

USPs are a familiar concept in sales. In a supermarket, faced with all those breakfast cereals, why choose the one you do? You do so because of the USPs that you think it has. Companies spend a lot of money ensuring that their brand and their packaging are unique in some way. In preparation for your interview make sure that you spend a lot of time thinking about yourself as a brand, what will make you special and/or the ideal candidate for this position. You develop these achievements to create your USPs. In this way you can become a brand and, as you know from your supermarket shopping, the appropriately positioned brand has a far higher chance of being chosen.

Ask yourself the question: 'What is there in my experience or skills portfolio that is directly relevant to this position that the other candidates are unlikely to have?'

For instance for a computing job in a bank, the fact that you have a background in insurance will give you an edge over those other computer specialists on the short list who come from a background in retail, manufacturing or, say, mining because not only do you know about computing but you also know about financial systems and risk.

In your preparation for the interview develop four or five USPs specifically for the job on offer and weave them into your answers. Sometimes you get that gift of a question:

> **Why should I recruit you?**
> or
> **What makes you special?**

Now having FABed your achievements and worked on your USPs, questions like these will be a dream to answer. Not only that, you will also give the interviewer additional reasons to choose you from the short list.

LEARN THE ART OF STORYTELLING

An interesting feature of the brain is that it has a critical faculty which comes into play when listening to someone. With in-coming information, the listener is continually testing the information being received – does it sound right? Is it credible? Does it tally with what has been said before? Is it realistic? For some reason when listening to stories, this rigorous evaluation is considerably softened. Also the individual takes from the story what they want or need to hear. Perhaps this is one of the reasons why great religious teachers are remembered for their stories rather than their lectures.

In developing your stories make sure that they have a BSTAR structure where possible, where BSTAR stands for:

Benefit – The benefit to the organisation of what you did

Situation – The context and environment in which the main action takes place

Target – The target, KPIs or goals that needed to be achieved

Action – What you specifically did to achieve the target

Result – The direct outcome of what you did

In fact the BSTAR approach is an interviewing technique which is taught to many HR professionals, so you will actually be helping them do their job as well as being able to reduce the number of supplementary questions you get asked. Interviewers attempt to achieve 'Completed STARs' so that they gain a more accurate picture of your skills and abilities.

Because of our cultural inheritance people love to hear stories which have been an essential part of our learning whether round a camp fire or in front of a TV. Stories bridge the gap between theory and reality, between deductive and inductive thought processes. This being the case, develop stories about yourself and practice telling them. Not only will it make you more interesting, but your interviewer is likely to rate you higher on the demanded competencies.

There is another advantage. Put yourself in the place of the interviewer who might be seeing seven people one after the other all in one day. As candidates you are all similar because you are going for the same job and have roughly the same backgrounds and experience. It does not take long for you all to begin to merge together in the mind of the interviewer. It is like going to seven different McDonalds – they are all different yet all the same. When you tell interesting stories about yourself, you stand out from the crowd and are remembered. 'Oh he was the person who . . .'

EXPLAIN YOUR GAPS AND MOVES

What made you move from job to job is of great interest to your recruiter because it gives he or she an insight to your motivations, values and aspirations. You must ensure that you can explain why you left a position and what attracted you to the next post without saying anything that could be construed as negative or detrimental towards the job for which you are currently being interviewed.

INTERVIEW YOURSELF

This is quite simple – if you were going to recruit someone for the job you're going for, what questions would you ask and what sort of person would you want? Now just devise a list of questions and prepare your answers.

PREPARE FOR THE CHALLENGES

In reality, no candidate is perfect and there are going to be some things missing in your experience or qualifications that the employer would like to have in the ideal candidate. Look at what is weak or missing in your application and then prepare positive answers and justifications for them in case you are challenged. (Beware of 'white elephanting' yourself here – see page 11).

BE POSITIVE

No surprises here. Interviewers take more notice of negative information than positive. Negative information also attracts more supplementary questions, so always give positive information. We call this 'staying above the line'. Below the line is the negative stuff and above the line is the positive. If the interviewer takes you below the line then dwell on it as briefly as possible and take the interviewer back up above the line with a phrase like: 'It was good because I then went on to . . .' or: 'What I learnt was . . . and this enabled me to . . .' Hopefully the rapport needs of the interviewer will keep him or her on the new positive topic that you have just introduced.

A WORD OF WARNING

As you would expect, this little book gives you examples of how to answer interviewers' questions and that is probably why you made the investment. Now here is the danger – you could ask a lot of HR people and professional recruiters what the best answer to a question might be and every one of them would give a different answer. This is because we are all different and we all have different needs and experiences. So here I have to misquote Abraham Lincoln by saying:

> **Most of the example answers here will work most of the time with most of the interviewers. But not all of the answers will work all of the time with all of the interviewers.**

However, through our work in our Career Consultancy

both in Europe and the Asia Pacific region and through our research and contact with many recruitment specialists, we are confident that the examples will work for the majority of situations, or at least the principles behind them will. Treat the examples as off-the-peg answers to which you are going to have to do some individual tailoring so that they fit you perfectly. After all, you want the interviewer to hire you, not someone who can memorise answers. And so we come to the next danger:

DO NOT ATTEMPT TO LEARN THESE ANSWERS PARROT FASHION

This will not help you at all. It will be obvious to the interviewer and what are you going to do when you are asked a question which is not covered in this book?

Please also be realistic. After one of my interviewing workshops in Glasgow, I was tackled by a man during a follow-up session. He challenged me saying that he could not have complete confidence in my training because he specifically remembered that the interviewer for a recent job interview did not ask him questions 34, 52 and 90 from the coursework book.

Now lets look at the type of questions that you might get asked.

What sort of questions?

The interview is built around questions, so if you can predict what sort will be thrown at you, you will be better placed to respond appropriately. A good interviewer will only speak for about 10% of the time because to be able to make an appropriate decision about your employability you should be doing most of the talking. This being so, you need to be able to control the process as much as possible and the skill of being able to classify questions as they get asked will be to your advantage.

THE 'SUPER QUESTION'

Before you start to classify questions, there is a 'super question' you should ask yourself: 'Why am I being asked this question?' The interviewer is trying to assess you as a potential employee so this is not a social situation. Behind every question there is a specific requirement of the job on offer that needs to be satisfied. Your task, through your answers, is to reduce the risk of the interviewer so that he or she feels confident offering you the job. Of course interviewers do not ask questions to which they already know the answers, such as 'Can you can read or write?' – that is assumed. Interviewers only ask a question where there is a doubt over whether or not you have the skills, ability and experience to do the job. This is why you ask yourself the super question before you answer any question. In other words, 'What is the question behind this question?' or 'What does the interviewer want to hear?' As useful as it is to be able to be confident and fluent, unless you can unpack the reasons behind the questions, your application is likely to be a bit of a lost cause.

THE SAFE QUESTIONS FIRST

Questions are like people – they come in all shapes and sizes. Some are easy to get on with but others need caution and need to be approached carefully. Here are some of the 'families' of questions that you are likely to encounter.

Closed questions
These are a gift to you. Closed questions are those that can be answered with a straightforward 'Yes' or 'No'. These are gifts because they provide a unique opportunity for you to gain the advantage by expanding your answer in any way you wish with a simple, 'Yes and . . .' or 'No and . . .' After which you can take the interviewer into the territory of your experience and achievements that promote your skills for the position you want.
Example:

Do you enjoy working as part of a team?

You could give the simple answer: 'Yes I do', but you short-change yourself so harvest the opportunity you have been given:

> Yes I do, especially when I can make a specific contribution from my skills. When I was working at xxx my contribution was xxx and it was very satisfying in that we achieved xxx on time and to budget in spite of all the difficulties. It was a real team effort.

You will know when you have a trained interviewer because they rarely ask closed questions. However, even with professionals it is surprising how closed questions slip out for you to catch and use to your advantage.

As soon as you get bowled a closed question, be ready to go where you want to go and hope that it encourages the interviewer to stay in territory that you are happy to explore together because of its relevance to the job.

Hypothetical questions

This is another bonus for you. Hypothetical questions come packaged as 'What would you do if . . .' There is a huge difference between what you have done and what you would do. Who knows what you would do in any circumstance because there are so many variables.

So when presented with a hypothetical question there is a golden opportunity for you to provide the perfect answer and say whatever you think is most appropriate as that is what you might do and not what you will do.

Example:

What would you do to increase sales?

Answer:

I would conduct an analysis of our current client base to see why they buy from us and what our unique selling propositions are. Then identify the demographics to pre-select ideal prospects. My next strategy would be market research so we could gain some hard data on the direction of the market . . .

That is the answer but who really knows what you would do; because, although it sounds impressive, it is all hypothetical really.

There is another advantage to hypothetical. It comes from our knowledge of the sales process and they are called buying questions. In asking a hypothetical question the interviewer – who is buying you – is projecting you into an actual work situation to see how you would respond to their particular environment. He or she is actually projecting you in his or her mind into the job and attempting to calculate how well you would do in the position.

For example, the organisation may be having difficulty with cash flow so you might be asked: 'How would you encourage clients to pay more quickly?'

The interviewer is not going to ask out of pure curiosity, but because it is a current or future problem that the organisation is dealing with. So rejoice and be glad the implication is that you are in the process of being bought – you just have to satisfy your interviewer in the details and close the deal!

Rhetorical questions

Again these are a gift from the interviewer for you to capitalise on. With every rhetorical question comes a huge cue card above the interviewer's head telling you exactly what you are supposed to say.

Example:

You can work shifts can't you?

What are you going to say here? 'No I can't and I'm only going to work for the contractual hours you pay me for and even less if I can get away with it.' The huge cue card in large print above the interviewer's head suggests you should say:

> Yes, of course, I worked shifts when I was with xxx and having discussed this important aspect with my wife and family they are right behind me in their support and we have made the necessary domestic arrangements. In fact as I have an interest in xxx, shift work is very attractive to me because I can do more of xxx.

Other questions of this type could include:

- **How flexible are you?**
- **Can you cope with pressure?**
- **Are you a team person?**
- **Can you travel?**

And how you answer them is so obvious we will move on.

Multiple Questions
Many interviewers make the easy mistake of thinking through their questions whilst they are still asking them. This means that they ask a question and then change it before you have had a chance to reply. So do not be

surprised if you are asked three or even four questions at the same time. What a gift! This is like an exam where you only have to answer three questions out of ten and, better still, you get the choice of which question illustrates best your candidacy by choosing to answer the question which reveals your skills and achievements.

Example:

What sort of firm was xxx ... er ... tell me what did you like about xxx ... er ... I mean from the point of view of what was important for the job ... such as what you felt you wanted to do?

So here you have four things you can talk about:

- What sort of firm ...
- What you liked ...
- What was important ...
- What you wanted to do ...

Your choice. How easy. Have fun!

Alternative choices
Now these are slightly more difficult but you can still convert them to your advantage. Have you ever had a salesperson place you in what in technical terms is called 'a bind' or in sales terms 'the alternative close'? It goes like this: 'When can I come and see you; which would be more convenient for you, this week or next?' The question is presented as a choice but in the subtext there is no choice – you are going to be seen either this week or next week!

So with alternative choice you are only given a couple of alternatives and expected to respond.

Example:

What did you like about xxx, was it the work or the people?

Now in fact what you really liked about xxx was the money, the status, the power, the international tours and the fat expense account, I joke but in all seriousness you would reply:

It is difficult if you give me an either/or because I would really prefer it to be a both/and. The work really gave me an opportunity to use my skills in xxx and I had great fun working with a really good team of fellow professionals. Would it be helpful if I gave you a specific example?

NOW THE DANGEROUS QUESTIONS

Open questions

Open questions are just that. They begin with 'How', 'What' and 'Why' or even 'Tell me . . .' They are dangerous because what you choose to talk about and the way you order the topics tells the interviewer so much about you.

Take the simple question: 'What did you like about xxx company?' Now you are in difficulty because the question is so wide you could fly a 747 through it. You could talk about the technology, the financial structure, the product, the people, the culture, the market and tens of other aspects about xxx company. We will cover how to answer these questions in some depth later.

Behavioural questions

These questions are like lasers that lock onto your past behaviour and compare it with a specific competency demanded by the job. You know when you are the recipient that you are going to be worked over by a professional.

Behavioural questions are based on the premise that what you have done in the past is the best indicator of future work behaviour. They are the opposite of hypothetical questions. Here the interviewer is holding your past behaviour over a template of what the behaviour in the new job requires.

You know when you are getting a behavioural question and a trained interviewer when you get asked:

- Tell me about a time when you . . .
- Specifically, what did you do on the xxx project?
- How did you close the xxx sale?

Now it's not all doom and gloom. Advantageous to you is the fact that in every behavioural question you get asked, a competency that the organisation is looking for or is required by the job is given away. You then know what they are looking for and you can give – providing you are well prepared, having done your achievement list – the example which shows you have the experience required.

Behavioural questions are very similar to a system called Competency Interviewing to which we now turn.

Competency questions

This is a very popular form of interviewing with trained professionals because it is very effective. It is sometimes known as targeted interviewing. It is mainly used for management and executive positions, although more and more it is being used for all types of jobs. It does not matter what your function, speciality or profession is because the questions are constructed around the generic identified needs of the organisation as well as those of the job. Competency interviewing places a heavy weight on your experience and what you have specifically achieved in your working life.

Competency interviewing tends to be rather boring for the interviewer because most of the questions have the same type of introduction as a prefix, including:

- Tell me about a time when . . .
- What have you done in . . . ?
- Outline your experience in . . .
- How did you approach . . . ?

Also since the interviewer has to cover seven or so competences in the time available rapport certainly suffers as you are bounced from one competency to another.

The advantage for the selector is that it keeps you, the applicant, rooted in what you have done with the interviewer focusing on the fact that, 'if you have done it for them you can do it for me'. This is why it is so important to have completed your achievement list well before you go for interviews.

But this system of interviewing brings a definite advantage to you as the interviewee. Interviewers have to ask a targeted question and consequently it is very difficult for them to disguise what they are looking for. Should you get several questions around teamwork and initiative then you know that these areas are essential to the position on offer and can tailor your answers accordingly. It also means that you must amend your career statement which you are going to use at the end of the interview – see page 70.

Now we can examine the basic competencies that most employers are going to be looking for.

The major competencies

Any job, irrespective of whether you are tea person or chairperson, will require some of the following competencies. In preparation for your interview you would do well to go through your achievement list and see which items demonstrate the points below. As a preparation activity you might like to turn all these points into potential interview questions and test yourself.

As you will see there can be a fair amount of over-lap in these example competencies but your achievement list should ensure that you can give a variety of illustrations.

TEAM ORIENTATION

In your preparation for the interview you could think through how you would demonstrate some of the following from your work history:

- Being able to work with and support others
- Being willing to co-operate with others
- Being able to work within a role

- Being able to sacrifice personal objectives for those of the team
- Being able to encourage others
- Being able to accept direction from fellow team members
- Being able to work to consensus decisions
- Being able to minimise conflict
- Being able to publicly support a position with which you disagree

For example:

- Tell me about the team you currently work with and how you see your role.
- How have you gone about putting a team together – besides technical competence what other factors do you consider?
- Tell me about a time when a team took a decision with which you did not agree.

Interpersonal ability
- Being able to get on with people who hold different views and/or values to yourself
- Being able to control your emotions
- Being able to listen to others
- Being able to influence others to your viewpoint
- Being able to perceive the needs of others
- Being able to achieve win/win situations

For example:

- Tell me about a time when it was necessary for you to control your emotions in a work situation.
- When did you last encourage a colleague to change his or her mind?

- Give me an example of when you had to coach or mentor one of your staff.
- What was the result of a recent negotiation you have had and how was it achieved?

SELF-MANAGEMENT

- Being able to take personal responsibility for both your successes and your failures
- Being able to act honestly and with integrity
- Being able to manage your time effectively
- Being able to prioritise your work
- Being able to show initiative
- Being able to be flexible and change if required
- Being able to fulfil the commitments that you make to others
- Being able to act assertively when necessary

For example:

- Tell me about a time when you had to let someone down.
- How have you prepared for this interview?
- What criteria do you use to prioritise your work?
- What is the biggest work decision you've made to date without referring your action to a higher authority?
- Tell me about a time when you had to be assertive.

SPECIFIC COMPETENCIES

What follows are specific competencies with their definitions that an organisation will be looking for, together with typical questions and, where possible, suggested answers. The definitions are very general and to be taken as examples only. Also the answers will have to be tuned to your specific situation and that is why they are 'example questions' rather than 'sample questions'.

You will be relieved to know that it is highly unlikely that you will have an interview that will attempt to cover all the competencies that are outlined here. Give some thought to the position you are going for then select five or six that will apply to you and correlate them with your achievements.

Conceptual Ability

This is the ability to comprehend and process information in both a structured and creative way, analysing data and using critical reasoning.

For example:

- **Describe a major problem you dealt with recently.**
  - What were the major components of the problem?
  - What options did you consider?
  - What option did you eventually select and why?
- **What are the major problems faced by your industry today?**
- **How has the market changed in the past five years?**

Example answer:

The major challenge for the market, from my perspective, has come from two fronts really. First taking advantage of globalisation and second how to maximise that huge commercial opportunity with the technology before the competition which has always been strong in . . . In the case of my industry the specifics were that . . . which lead to . . . which in retrospect because of . . . was not perhaps the best option with the result that . . . however, it did mean that . . .

Managing change

This is the ability to identify opportunities for change which improve the business and/or performance and be able to implement them in a meaningful way.

For example:

- Tell me about a change that you have initiated during the last two years.
  - What was the opportunity?
  - What challenges did you face in making the change?
  - What was it about the change that was difficult for you personally?
- What specifically can you do now, that you could not do two years ago?

Example answer:

The real drive that I wanted to implement was to change the orientation of my department from being process-orientated to being customer driven. Coming from an engineering background it was a real challenge since, to be successful, it was going to have to be a 'people thing'. I could change the systems but it really had to be a 'hearts and minds' project. It meant giving individuals more responsibility and encouraging them to be flexible rather than bound by our processes. What I did was . . . and it was not easy because . . . It certainly tested and developed my management skills. What I learnt from the whole experience was . . . Was it successful? Well yes because the approach I developed was used as a model for other departments in the company.

Flexibility
This is being able to work in different and changing environments or, where there is a high degree of ambiguity, managing to change work priorities when necessary.
For example:

- Please tell me about a time when your work was disrupted by unforeseen circumstances.
  - What actions did you take?
  - What did you enjoy and what did you find difficult?
- When did you last change your mind over a significant business proposition?
- What do you do differently now at work than, say, two years ago?

Example answer:

Over the last two years there have been some significant changes I have dealt with in three areas, mainly: technology, market orientation and changes in the organisation structure. Changes in technology have enabled us to . . . which has been particularly beneficial when the market emphasis shifted towards . . . Last year we had another organisational restructure which meant doing more with less and this came on top of those other changes. All in all it was an exciting and challenging time.

Communications

This is the ability to express concepts, ideas and information so that they are understood by others in a way that is acceptable to them.

For example:

- **Tell me about a presentation you made.**
  - What went well?
  - What would you improve for next time?
- **Tell me about a time when you found it difficult to explain something to someone.**
- **What was the most challenging report you ever had to make?**
  - Why was it difficult?
  - Which of your skills did you find most useful?
  - What, if anything, did you achieve?

Example answer:

> One of the most testing presentations I had to make was on the technical aspects of one of our products to a client audience. Some of whom were highly technical, but there were also senior people there who were the real decision makers who were more interested in what our product would do, rather than how it worked. I devised some clever schematics showing how the technology delivered and supported the benefits. In spite of all my preparation and pre-runs, on the actual day the gremlins got hold of the PowerPoint at the end of the presentation but with some quick thinking I was able to ad lib my way through to a successful conclusion in that we got the business.

Motivating people

This is the ability to ensure that people perform as well as they can, most of the time.

For example:

- Give me an example of when you improved the performance of your subordinate/team/colleagues.
- Tell me how you ensured that someone took more responsibility at work.
- Tell me about the poorest performer you ever had to manage.
  - What did you do?
  - What was the result?

Example answer:

> Everyone is motivated by something – it is just a case of finding the key that turns them on. Most people are motivated by genuine praise and recognition but sometimes you just have to use your experience. One of my people had to do a daily return which was important but boring to do and he would avoid it if he could or procrastinate. We talked it through and I discovered that he was doing what he liked most first and leaving the stuff he did not like to last. Having thought about this I suggested that his priority order was making his work hard for him. If he reversed the order and did the worst first then each task would be more enjoyable and the day would get better as he worked through what he had to do. This was a revelation to him and he never missed a report thereafter.

Coaching and Mentoring

This is the ability to identify shortfalls in an individual's performance and develop that person so they can work to a satisfactory level.

For example:

- Tell me about a time when you had to assist a new colleague in 'learning the ropes'.
- Tell me about a time when you took advantage of a coaching opportunity.
- How did you specifically help a colleague through a difficulty at work?

Example answer:

People learn in different ways and at different speeds. Some learn by doing and some by thinking or reading. I have found it best to present the learning opportunity in a way that best suits the individual. For example . . . [here you tell a story] . . . Two more things are important. First it is rare that someone gets it right first time, so you have to provide a safe environment which can tolerate small mistakes and errors; and secondly it is important to ensure that there are opportunities in their work to practice and develop their new skill.

Achieving Results

This is the ability to be action orientated, ensuring that KPIs are satisfied.

For example:

- Why does your job exist?
- What have you specifically achieved this month?
- Tell me about a time when you did not have the resources to do your job properly.

This is a golden opportunity to use your achievement list and present what you did in a BSTAR format – see page 34.

Quality orientation

This is the ability to produce good quality work and a desire to maintain high standards.

For example:

- How do you ensure quality in your work?
  - Give me an example.
- Tell me about a time when you had to pay attention to detail.
- Have you ever been asked to improve the quality of your work?
  - What was the situation?
  - What did you do about it?
- How do you monitor the work of your team?

Example answer:

> Quality is paramount. It is what keeps customers loyal, it minimises rework and in one's own work it leads to recognition and promotion. Quality has a cost, of course, but it is important to meet customer expectations, whether they are external or internal. At our monthly meetings there is always a quality review agenda item. It was because of my concern for quality that . . . [tell your story] . . .

Initiative

This is the ability to identify a need or business opportunity and take the appropriate steps to maximise your advantage.

For example:

- How have you improved a situation or process?
- What is the most original thing you have done at work?
- Tell me about a time when you took the initiative on something at work.

Example answer:

> When I first took the job I undertook a rigorous examination of the processes. To my surprise several were totally redundant and there were some, such as quarterly appraisals, missing. Although I knew what was necessary I organised discussions with those involved as to how we could improve our processes. No surprises – we dropped the redundant requirements introduced the quality checks and productivity rose by 7.5% and re-work time dropped by 11.2%. It was good to get a success under my belt so early in the job.

Supplementary questions

Supplementary questions are questions that probe your answers to check veracity or to gain more information. It is an interviewing skill called 'funnelling'. Using an innocuous open question the interviewer puts your answer through a funnel and then keeps probing – i.e. pushing you down the funnel until, at the end of the funnel, you disclose what you specifically did and the results achieved. Your answer is then held up against a required competency for the position, so that your skill, experience or behaviour can be evaluated either in its own right or against the other candidates. See Figure 1 on page 61.

Typical supplementary questions would be:

- Please give me an example of that.
- When was that?
- What specifically happened?
- What did you actually do?
- Why did you take that approach?
- What was the result?
- How was that received?
- Tell me how that came about.
- And what was the result?

This is where preparation is so important. Think of whatever you say in response to a question as a target that the interviewer can legitimately shoot at as often as he or she wishes. Advice here is obvious; do not say anything unless you can speak about it at length and what you say has a direct bearing on the job on offer. Why is it, do you think, that police forces throughout the democracies of the world say: 'You have the right to remain silent'?! Do not incriminate yourself by saying something in response to a question that you cannot justify, provide an example for, or tell a story about. This is one of the reasons we spend so much time 'FABing' our achievements. See page 31.

SNEAKY SUPPLEMENTARY QUESTIONS

Professional interviewers are skilled at getting more information out of you than perhaps you would wish to give, or taking you where you would rather not go. Here are a couple of tricks and strategies they use:

Key word repetition
Interestingly this type of questioning technique comes not from selection but from the realms of psycho-therapy. Key word repetition is a powerful tool because questions appear innocuous and innocent but in reality are very invasive. Therapists use it because it is an excellent way of opening up a client in a sensitive area. Professional interviewers soon realised that they could employ this type of questioning to encourage candidates to talk about aspects of their work which they would prefer to be silent about.

Here is an example of key word questioning in action:

Figure 1

FUNNELLING

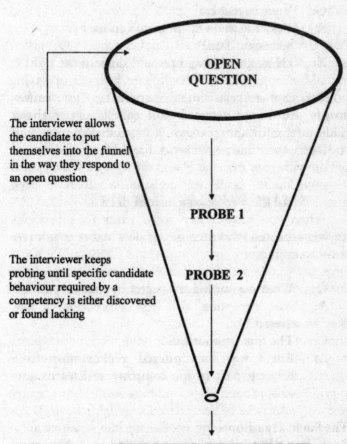

OPEN QUESTION

The interviewer allows the candidate to put themselves into the funnel in the way they respond to an open question

PROBE 1

The interviewer keeps probing until specific candidate behaviour required by a competency is either discovered or found lacking

PROBE 2

SPECIFIC BEHAVIOUR

Your specific behaviour is then matched against the required competency

Q: 'Why are you thinking of leaving your present employer?'

A: 'Because I am not getting on too well with my manager.'

Q: 'Your manager?'

A: 'Yes, it is the way he speaks to me.'

Q: 'Speaks to you?'

A: 'He keeps making personal suggestions.'

You can see here what is happening. Just the key words are being repeated and this is drawing out additional information on what is a sensitive subject. If the interviewer had just asked a direct, 'Why did you not get on with your manager?' and the interviewee was still sensitive on the issue, the question would have been avoided and the wrong conclusions drawn.

When you have a key word from your previous answer repeated you can now decide whether or not you want to go there.

Q: 'What is your biggest regret in your career?'

A: 'Not accepting the first promotion I was offered.'

Q: 'The first promotion?'

A: 'But I was then offered a promotion to a different part of the company and learnt new skills in xxx.'

The Silent Question

As we have already commented, it is interesting that most of the police forces within democracies say, 'You have the right to remain silent'. Now the reason you get given this option is that the more you say the more likely you are to entrap yourself. It is just the same in the selection interview. If you get trapped into saying more than you wish to, then you might talk yourself out of a job.

How is it done? You get a simple question and after you have answered it the interviewer just stays silent and looks at you. In body language terms your interviewer is saying, 'Please go on and tell me more'. If you are not careful you will do just that and entrap yourself by saying too much, saying something that you did not prepare for or 'white elephanting' yourself. (For white elephanting see page 11.)

Remember that silence is golden for interviewers because it gives them so much information when used against an interviewee.

The one-word invitation

Occasionally just single words are used to the same effect as silence. Such words are subtle invitations, simply saying, 'Tell me more'.

For example:

- **Interesting.**
- **Really?**

These simple single words encourage you to go on and, of course, if you are not careful, you simply dig a bigger hole for yourself.

Para-language

Sometimes there is a variation on the silent or one-word treatment which is known as 'para-language' – like paramilitary or paralegal it means similar but not quite the same.

We use para-language in our everyday conversation, but professional interviewers are trained to use it to their advantage. What are these para-language words? Non-words such as:

- Ah ha
- Umm

The nonsense words really mean: 'Go on tell me more'. Sometimes these sounds are called 'minimisers' or 'encouragers' but, whatever their technical term, when you hear them alarm bells should go off in your head. Umm . . . you should be aware!

How to plan for questions

BE THE INTERVIEWER

You do not have to be a Nobel Prize winner to work out what questions you might get asked. Just play the part of the interviewer and ask yourself who would be the ideal candidate and what questions would you want to ask them. The interview is not like meeting someone socially; it is a structured event with definite defined objectives. So thinking about how you would structure the interview if the roles were reversed is a good way to anticipate the questions that you might get asked.

WHAT IS THE BUZZ?

Jobs exist not only within organisations, but within a competitive context of technology and market place. This means that similar organisations offering similar products and/or services will be facing the same types of problems and enjoying the same sorts of opportunities. This has a distinct advantage for you and can provide you with an excellent inside edge. All you have to do is use your network to find someone who is already in a similar position to the one you are going for, preferably in the same industry or sector. This is because of the way that capitalism works, their problems and opportunities will be similar to the job you are going for. By getting information from them not only will you have a better idea of the job but also a better idea of how you might approach it and which aspects of your achievements will be immediately of interest to your interviewer and relevant to your application.

If you don't have anyone in your network who can help or refer you, do not worry, just ring the person you have identified and tell him or her that you are doing some research into the field (which of course you are) and would he or she be happy to answer a few simple questions. Most people are incredibly obliging and generous with their time.

Professional journals and magazines
Use of the professional media can be exceptionally helpful in discovering what is the 'flavour of the month and the flame of the hour'. Not only do problems and opportunities do the rounds but so do corporate initiatives; remember the pursuit of excellence? Then it was JIT management, then vision statements, then re-engineering, then downsizing then rightsizing, then creating added value and there will be lots of 'ings' to come – commerce is just another fashion victim. The fashion cycles might be longer but they are still there and you will be expected to know the latest management fad and how it affects your position, your function and your sector. Journals help you with this, since most of their articles are written by consultants hoping their thing will become the next big thing.

The business pages

You will already, if you have read the sister book *Perfect CV*, be reading the business pages of the media with the mindset, 'Who can give me a job?' Business pages also give you a backdrop to what is happening and reading them regularly will help you understand and answer questions about the context of your potential job and the financial environment in which your sector operates. If, for example, it is a global company manufacturing in the UK but selling to the USA then the pound/dollar relationship is going to be of significance. Is the organisation, for instance, trying to expand its business into regions in which the West is not politically popular? How do moves toward free trade or the reverse affect your company? By reading the business pages you will soak up this information and, if questioned, your knowledge will add a richness and a breadth to your answers. It also relates back to the 'helicopter view' substantiating your intellectual strengths. See page 20.

The fundamental rule of being interviewed

Do not answer interviewer's questions – respond to them!

A famous politician once greeted a press conference with the words, 'Good morning Ladies and Gentlemen, now which of you have questions for my answers?'

The politician, knowing what he wanted to say and the points he wanted to make, ensured that he was going to respond to questions rather than answer them. In your pre-interview planning you will have thought about your achievements and those aspects of your background which match the requirements of the job. With these in the forefront of your mind you are more likely to be able to weave your star points into your answers. This is what we mean by responding to questions.

When you get asked a question by the interviewer your mind can go through an internal process like this:

- Do I understand the question?
- Why am I being asked the question?
- To which competency required by the job does it refer?

- Out of the whole range of all my experience what is the best or most appropriate answer?
- How can I illustrate what I want to say through a quantified work achievement of mine that had a specific benefit to my employer?
- How can I present my answer in an enthusiastic way which will be easily understood by the interviewer?

This might seem like a tall order but once you practice answering questions you will be amazed at how easy it is to respond by giving the most appropriate answer rather than the exact or precise answer.

THE STOCK QUESTIONS

One can never predict precisely what questions you are going to get in an interview but there are some which are fairly generic to most situations, irrespective of the job you are going for. You would do well to prepare for all these questions but do not be disappointed if you do not get them all.

Many of the questions here are typical of those you will be asked by the HR person and you will see they are more to do with you as a person rather than your technical abilities. This is bound to be so because HR will not be able to challenge you in terms of your technical expertise and thus will be more interested in you and what motivates you.

It does not matter whether you are a recent graduate, a returner, someone who has suffered redundancy or just a regular job-hunter, these are what I would call stock questions. (You might do well to tack these questions onto the section later in the book that is appropriate for your particular situation.)

1. Why have you applied for this position?
or

What was it about the advert that appealed to you?
Now you might want to get away from a horrible boss, or you think that your company is going down the tubes faster than a monkey on a slippery pole, but follow the basic rule of not answering the question but responding to it so that you help the interviewer move onto areas which make you attractive and the better candidate.

For example:

Well the advert suggested that the position would require someone to be able to do xxx well and that has always been the part of the position I have enjoyed the most . . .

Having developed skills in xxx and discovered that I gain a great deal of satisfaction from doing xxx this seemed like a progressive career opportunity.

2. Tell me about yourself.
This is an absolute gift of a question and it is surprising how many candidates throw this opportunity away. Of course it is a huge open question and can be answered in a huge number of ways. In reality the interviewer wants to know who and what you think you are.

There is also a hope that the question will provide a significant number of topics that can be pursued at leisure and in depth later in the interview. Also what you say now will be expected to be consistent with what you say later in the discussion.

How do you tackle this key question? Well, before going for any job you need to say to yourself:

If candidates were only allowed 30 to 40 words to

describe themselves and this was all the information that a prospective employer had before the hire decision was made, what would I say about myself?

This approach keeps you focused on why you are sitting in a chair and letting a stranger ask you questions about yourself.

Surprisingly, when asked this question candidates frequently respond with the counter question: 'Do you mean at home or at work?' How dumb! Anyone can talk about themselves at great length without mentioning anything directly relevant to the job on offer. This does not help the interviewer or, more importantly, you the applicant.

The interviewer wants to know about you primarily in the work setting, you could talk for hours about yourself outside work but it is unlikely that you would cover the competencies that would give you pole position for the job. Using the advert, your knowledge of the job and the industry and information culled from your network, develop a specification for the job on offer and then develop your statement.

Do yourself an enormous favour and develop what is called a career statement. This is 30 to 40 words that sum you up as a potential employee. A strong career statement immediately creates a powerful and appropriate impression exactly when you want it: right at the beginning of the interview. Just as a good book, film or speech should provide a strong and engaging opening, your interview should have a great start with the judicious use of a powerful career statement.

Here are some examples responding to the question: 'Tell me about yourself':

I am an experienced secretary who is used to

working in partnership with the team. I have proven administration and organisational abilities supported by good interpersonal skills.

I am an experienced bilingual industrial designer with an extensive knowledge of the automotive industry. My track record suggests that I have strong aesthetic skills and a good understanding of commercial reality.

I am a self-motivated and achievement-orientated financial controller who has strong business development skills and a proven record of profit improvement through planning and implementing financial and MIS strategies.

Here are some more examples but with a softened and not so prominent 'I am':

As you can see from my CV I am an experienced customer service person with good administrative and keyboard skills. People say that I have a quiet personality and that I am good on administrative detail.

As I hope to have demonstrated on my application, I am an experienced management accountant with an extensive career in the retail and leisure industry. I have strong business development skills and a proven record of profit improvement through planning and implementing financial and MIS strategies.

In terms of my career I am an industrial designer with an in-depth knowledge of the automotive industry. I have particularly strong aesthetic skills

combined with a developed understanding of manu-facturing requirements and commercial reality.

Now this might all sound like boasting, but please remember that in an interview you are expected to boast as long as you do not tell lies.

Now here are some further tips to succeed with answering this question: First of all write out your answer again and again until you have honed all the words and made your statement as brief as possible. Would the statement make you the ideal candidate? If not, do more work on it.

Now learn the statement off by heart so that you can repeat it easily without too much thinking. This is dangerous because if you answer this question too quickly, the interviewer will know that either you have been trained in interviewing skills or think that you have been to so many interviews in the last few months that you can anticipate the question. In both of these situations alarm bells go off in the interviewer's head. So, next, practice acting the answer as if you were delivering it for the very first time. For example:

Pause – to show that you are thinking – then: **'Well I am a technically aware sales co-ordinator.'** Pause, look at the interviewer's desk, then continue: **'My boss says that I am good at controlling multiple marketing projects,'** pause and look somewhere else, **'because I think it is important to keep within agreed timescales'**, pause, look at another part of the room and conclude by saying: **'and I suppose I am pretty good at keeping salespeople to their commitments.'** Conclude by looking at the interviewer and if appropriate smile.

The reason why there is all this looking away is because when you are thinking, 'you work behind the eyes'. If you want to see this in action just watch someone as they are speaking on the telephone – their eyes move all over the place but they are not 'looking'.

Much research suggests that the interviewer makes up his or her mind about a candidate in the first four minutes of the interview, so if this question comes early it is a real gift because it preconditions the interviewer into thinking that you are a strong candidate and candidates thought to be good get an easier interview than those who appear suspect. Yes, the interview is an unfair process.

So this is what to do with your career statement:

Write it, Craft it, Learn it, Act it

(*Perfect* CV goes into greater detail on how to create a 30–40 word career statement and gives some examples too.)

3. Why do you want this job?

Any employer will want to know this and you should be pretty clear as well. Your answer will reveal not only what motivates you but also how strategic you are in planning your career as it moves forward. It is unlikely that you would be taken on just because you did not have a job or because you were financially strapped for cash.

Your USPs would be ideal here to make you that special candidate – see page 33.

This position offers me the opportunity to use my skills in xxx and put my experience to good use. It is also a step towards a long-term career within your company.

> This position attracts me because it offers variety and your organisation is of interest because it enjoys a reputation for being a good employer.

> I am interested in this position because it is the next logical step in my career and being a progressive company I am sure that there will be opportunities if I work hard and do well.

4. How do you like to get things done at work?

This question is testing your preferred style and addressing the point that people not only need to do the job well, but also they need to fit into the organisation.

It is a hypothetical question so you have quite a bit of license to expand on reality.

> I like to plan my day as much as possible and then be flexible within that to cover contingencies as they arise. Where possible I do the jobs I dislike or find boring first so the day becomes more enjoyable as it goes on. At the end of the day I reflect on how well I have done, possibly what I have learnt, and I set out my priorities for the next day.

5. What would a reference say about you?

If you have prepared properly you will have already briefed your referees about the job you are going for, the skills required, as well as reminding them of aspects of your experience which demonstrate those skills. You will also have given them a copy of your CV. Having done all this you can respond by outlining the key skills you have that are required by the job, confident that your referees will support your statement when the time comes.

You can add real force and credibility to your answer by starting off with:

I am sure if you picked up the phone and spoke to my boss she would say . . .

6. What environment do you work best in?
Again this is not to do with your skill and experience but more to do with fitting in. You will see that the suggested answer is very general because, unless you have real experience of it, you do not know what the prevailing environment is within the company.

An environment which allows me to work both as part of a team and make a personal contribution and be recognised for it. I also like to be challenged, so that I am growing both as a person and professionally. I am not the sort of person that needs close supervision but I like to be able to get advice and guidance when necessary.

7. How did you change the last job you had?
Jobs are never static for they change with technology and movements in the market but they are also changed by the style and approach of the incumbent. Your answer here will depend on what you actually did and will stand up to a telephone reference enquiry to your last boss. If you are really stuck try some thing bland along the lines of:

I helped to create a more friendly and co-operative atmosphere in my department by . . . which fostered team spirit, decreased absenteeism and boosted productivity.

8. What will you do if you do not get this position?

Do not worry, this question is not telling you indirectly that you are unlikely to get the job offer but rather to see what your plans are, and how committed you are to using the skills required in the job on offer. Respond appropriately by saying:

> I am committed to using my skills in xxx and yyy so I will do my best to join an organisation similar to yours which offers the same prospects and career opportunities. As you will imagine I have several applications out but I really want to join you because . . .

9. How have you changed over the last five years?

It is possible for someone to do the same job for 20 years and not to have 20 years' experience because they have just repeated the same year 20 times. Most employers will be more interested in someone who is growing and developing irrespective of where they are in their careers. If you have worked on your achievement list this should be an easy question for you to answer. The advice is to think through your recent achievements and match them up against the requirements of the job you are going for. All you have to do then is slant your answer as much as you can in that direction. Here is a possible framework for you:

> Five years ago I completed my degree/left xxx company. Since then, because I wanted to develop my career in xxx I self-funded my part-time studies in xxx. At work I managed to ensure that I gained experience in xxx which has been particularly useful in my field of xxx. Personally I feel I have grown, become more tolerant towards others and perhaps

more strategic in my approach to my career and life in general. Since having children my negotiation skills have been honed considerably.

My technology skills have improved considerably particularly in xxx. Also, I now know a great deal about SAP [or whatever is the 'in thing'] both in terms of theory and its implementation. I suppose with age comes wisdom and I certainly feel more confident. I have developed my professional skills and, of course, I have had the advantage of five years more experience especially in the area of xxx.

10. What are your weaknesses?

Perhaps this is the most dreaded question of them all and the one that confuses and confounds many. What do you say? 'None' and then they know that you are not particularly economic with the truth, or go belly up with total integrity, saying, 'Well as a matter of principle I take all my sickies.' Aso not recommended is: 'people used to say that I was arrogant but now I know I'm perfect'. Sometimes people attempt to get off the hook with humour through a one-word confession such as 'chocolate' or 'Kryptonite'. All very amusing but this will only win you a rye smile before this killer question gets asked of you again and you have already sent a warning signal to your interviewer that you are going to try and evade the answer.

We have already established that negative information draws a wake of supplementary questions which will take you below the line of acceptability. First go back to the golden rule of not answering the interviewer's questions but responding to them. That gets you off the direct-answer hook because you are now going to respond to the question by using a process that goes like this:

- Take a strength which is obvious about your disposition
- Tell a story about your distant past
- Show how your strength was a weakness
- Discuss how you overcame it and what you learnt from it
- Assert that the weakness no longer exists
- Stay quiet

Your answer should be something along the lines of:

Well I have always been an enthusiastic sort of person. In my first management job, which was ten or so years ago, I found that some of the quieter, reflective members of my team did not take well to me enthusing around them all the time. They wanted to be told what to do, by when, and given the resources. I learnt very quickly to manage people differently. I am still just as enthusiastic but my management style is tailored to the needs of the people I am working with.

Other examples could be:

I have always been very detail oriented but have trained myself to take a quick decision when necessary.

I like to be in control but have learnt that people need to be empowered to give of their best.

I am very competitive but recognise that at work you perform best when part of a team.

Putting the strength first softens the weakness and

provides the interviewer with something he or she wants. No one personality is perfect in every situation, for every strength in your dispositional profile there is a complimentary weakness. Genghis Khan, for example, had great powers of leadership but his merger and takeover policies were a little severe.

Now you have to be careful because the better interviewers will have invested in this book as well as you. So they might ask the weakness question in a different format. For example:

- **What aspect of your career would you change?**
- **If you were to do that project again how would you do it differently?**
- **What did you learn from doing xxx?**
- **How else would you have gone about xxx?**

At the end of your statement **STAY QUIET**. Although they have asked you about your weaknesses (plural) you are not going to volunteer more than just one. Why admit to aspects about yourself that are going to prevent you getting a job? If you are pressed then say something like: 'My partner always says I take my job too seriously', or 'There never seems to be enough hours in the day to do the work to the standard I want to do it.'

Only one person has ever come back to me and said that their interviewer smiled and said, 'You've been trained by Max Eggert!' and when my client confessed he had been tutored by me, the interviewer said, 'Yes, Max worked with me about three years ago.'

If the interviewer still comes back you can say something along the lines of:

I have really worked hard at thinking through what

my skills and strengths are and thought about what was required in this job before I applied. No one is perfect, but my track record and experience especially in xxx shows that I can make a significant contribution to this job. I hope that I am not being arrogant when I say that I really do think that my past achievements mean that I can make a positive contribution to this position.

You see again that you have not answered the interviewer's question but responded to it. However, if you choose this route, remember not to give such a response that could be construed as aggressive.

Questions for school leavers

Interviewers find interviewing school leavers the most difficult of all categories for lots of reasons. For example school leavers have little experience of work; they are often persuaded by their parents to go for careers which are not suitable for them; the age difference between the school leaver and the interviewer makes rapport difficult; and finally teenagers are not known for giving more than a one-word answer to an adult's question!

Here are some questions that attempt to tease out the ability and intelligence of school leaver applicants:

1. What was your favourite subject at school?
Usually the favourite subject is one that is easy for the student. Obviously the employer hopes that their most popular subject will be one that relates to the job on offer. Art and Music, for example, would not be the best choices if you were going into construction or banking.

A possible answer, if you cannot lead with an appropriate subject without telling a lie might be:

I was very fortunate in that I enjoyed all my subjects but if you forced me to choose, I would have to say

Art and Music because it was not difficult to do well in those subjects. What is satisfying is working hard at something like Maths and then having the sense of achievement of having done well.

2. Which subjects were easy for you and which were difficult?

What was easy and difficult reveals your natural abilities. Where you can, say subjects that relate to the job you are going for. Don't say which ones were difficult for you unless the interviewer asks you, saying something like: 'And the difficult subjects?' Unless you are going for a traineeship as a graphic artist you could attempt to get off the hook by smiling and saying, 'Well I have very little talent at art' and hope that the interviewer moves on to another topic.

For example:

I enjoyed all my subjects really. Of course from time to time there were challenges but you could always go to a teacher for additional help or my parents would help me.

The point here is that you are showing initiative by obtaining help and demonstrating persistence as one of your character traits.

3. Tell me about the best school project you ever did?

This provides an opportunity for you to show how you go about your work and how well organised you are.

For example:

I enjoyed most of my projects, they were fun to do and I usually achieved high marks for them. One I particularly enjoyed was on the solar system. I did all the research I could from the Internet, I also emailed NASA and they actually replied! The project also provided an opportunity for me to show off my computing skills as I integrated pictures and photographs into my presentation.

4. Where did you come in class?
This question is to find out how bright you are. You are lucky if you can say 'near the top', but if you can't, pick your best topic and say 'I usually came pretty high up in History and Geography.' You do not have to mention that in Maths you came near the bottom!

5. How did you prepare for your exams?
This is a question to discover three things about you: your motivation, your self-management discipline and organisational skills.

For example:

> We covered a great deal during the year so I decided to start my revision really early. I began with the hardest topics first so that as I revised, the subjects became easier. Sometimes it was difficult doing the revision as well as the homework but I knew that if I did not keep to my schedule I would begin to stress out and that is no way to prepare for exams if you want to be successful.

6. Tell me about your favourite teacher.
What is interesting about this question is that it gives an indication of the sort of person you enjoy working with and for. With a few supplementary questions, the interviewer might also gain an insight into the type of working environment and culture to which you would

be best suited. Unless it compromises you, a generic answer might be the most appropriate response.

For example:

> I got on with all my teachers, really. I liked Ms Hutton because she was always fair and considerate, Mr Smith was always helpful and Mr Bloggs made his subject really interesting. I can't say I had a favourite – I was fortunate in that all the staff were good.

7. What is your favourite TV show?

There is a real difference in people who watch sport, those who watch soaps and those who watch documentaries. A sweeping generalisation would be that sport suggests perhaps a competitive person; soaps, a people-oriented individual; and documentaries suggests someone interested in facts. A favourite show indicates what might satisfy the person and how they get on in a particular working environment. You have to remember that interviewers have very little to go on when you are a school leaver and, if they ask a question such as: 'What sort of environment do you like to work in?' you might get stumped because you do not understand the question or, if you do, you will be tempted to give them the answer they are looking for.

8. What sports do you like to play?

This is similar to the question above because there are individual sports such as athletics, and team sports such as soccer and netball. The danger is to say you like a sport when you don't – you will fall down on the supplementary questions! If you were a sports star at school then by all means promote yourself in terms of team orientation, discipline and competitiveness.

For example:

I really enjoy sports and I am good at most of them. My favourites are xxx and xxx and I have been fortunate enough to make the school teams in xxx and xxx. It is great to be part of a team – especially when we train hard and then win against a strong side.

If you are not a sports jock then the following might help:

I like most sports although I did not inherit the right genes to get into the school teams, but I do enjoy watching and I am a great supporter. That has been an advantage though in that I have been able to give more of my time to my studies which is difficult if you are a real sports star.

9. What have you read recently?

This is a favourite question so please make sure you have read something and you know both the title and the author as well as being able to provide an outline of the plot and some criticism. Also, recently means within the last three months! Do not lie. Murphy's Law states that if you say you have read something when you haven't, your interviewer will have read the book last week!

10. What do you like to do during the holidays?

Again this says something about you as a person. Cover all your bases by saying that you like to spend time with your family, friends and have some time to yourself.

For example:

I really enjoy my holidays. It is great to go away with

the family and have some quality time with them. I also have a wide circle of friends and it's good to catch up on all the gossip and do things with them, especially those who are not at school with me. Holidays are also when I get some 'me time' catching up on my stuff. Last summer I collated all my holiday photos and read some sci-fi.

11. Tell me about your hobbies/interests?

Here you give a similar style answer as you did for questions 7 to 10 above. If you can, show you are a well-rounded person by enjoying three main interest areas, namely: social, intellectual and sporting.

12. Have you ever had a part-time job?

If you have worked, the interviewer will probably ask you lots of supplementary questions on this topic because your experience and how you got on in a working environment will be a pretty good indicator of how you might get on in the job or training that is on offer. These questions could include: 'How did you get the job?', 'What do you like about it?', 'What sort of manager have you got?', 'What have you found difficult?' and 'What do you bring to your team?'

For example:

On Saturdays I work in a coffee shop which is good fun because I work with a great team of people, most of them much older than me. I like waitressing best because you get to meet all sorts of people and if I do well then I get good tips. Sometimes it is tiring being on your feet all day but it is very satisfying helping people enjoy themselves.

13. What will you spend your wages on?

Here you can show how sensible you are and how you plan.

For example:

> Music and clothes mostly, although I do save a regular amount and if I want something really special then I will save up for it. Last year I wanted a digital camera so I saved half and my dad put in half. This year I bought a scanner for my computer.

14. What do your parents do?

Sometimes parents have a great influence over what you do – especially in professions like law, medicine, the church and the armed services. It would also be interesting if your father drove a truck and you wanted to be a solicitor or vice versa.

Your exposure from your background could give you some idea of what to expect in a career. It is difficult to suggest an answer here but you can prepare one for yourself irrespective of whether the job you are going for is similar or different to that of your parents.

Here are some alternatives:

> Both my parents are lawyers, one is a solicitor the other a barrister and they were keen for me to follow their footsteps. But since my adolescence I have had a consuming passion for xxx so this is why I have applied to you because of your reputation in the field.

> My background is quite humble – my father being a ganger on building sites and my mother was a telephonist till she had children. I am fortunate in that they both valued education highly and have

really supported and encouraged my interest in xxx and, because of your reputation in the field, this is why I have applied to you.

15. What do your parents think about your working for us?

How much support you are going to get in the early days of your job is important. If your parents always dreamed you would be a solicitor and you want to get into the hospitality industry there may be some friction.

For example:

My parents have always been very supportive. I thought very hard about the career I wanted and discussed the pros and cons with my parents. Of course they know me very well and have given me some good advice. So to answer your question, I think they would be very proud of me should you give me the traineeship.

16. What results do you think you will get in your exams?

Now you are not going to shoot yourself in the foot and say 'Terrible!' But you also have to be humble.

For example:

Well, I have worked very hard – especially at xxx – so I am reasonably confident that I should do well but we will have to see. The important thing for me is that I know that I have done my best.

17. What offices did you hold – were you a prefect for example?

Behind this question lies a whole heap of assumptions

about leadership potential. Those pupils selected by the school staff to hold offices of this type are not likely to be deviant, difficult or highly individual – in other words, good corporate potential because, by and large, employers want employees, especially junior ones, to be willing, hardworking and compliant.

Being nominated for prefect is thought by some to indicate potential leadership skills but research has tended not to support this conclusion.

For example:

Yes I was made prefect – I was one of 12 from the 60 pupils in my year. I thought it would be difficult directing fellow pupils but it worked out fine, in fact it was quite enjoyable. The fact that I could escape to the prefects' room when I wanted some time out was a distinct advantage.

We were fortunate in having many extra-curricular activities made available to us, being interested in xxx I was an active member of the xxx Society which I enjoyed very much.

18. Why did you choose this industry/sector/type of job?

This is an opportunity for you to promote some of your talents whether they are technical or based on your personality.

For example:

Maths and the sciences have always been easy for me and I enjoy them. I am also a pretty down-to-earth sort of person so working in a laboratory would suit me very well because I would be working with real things, there would be procedures and, hopefully, I could use my maths in some way.

I have always been a people person and helping others gives me great satisfaction. So being a nurse really appeals. I appreciate that it is hard work and sometimes you are working under difficult conditions but I am confident that it is the right area for me.

In addition, employers are interested in what makes their industry of interest to young people. They also want to know how you made the decision or what specifically influenced you. This question could provide you with an opportunity to show what sort of person you are so here is a possible answer:

I have always been interested in xxx and it is important for me to have a job which is both interesting and challenging. I also want a career in an area where there are going to be opportunities to develop myself and in which I can build on my strengths.

If you know someone in the industry you might wish to add something along the lines of:

My father/uncle/friend works in the industry/sector/ area as an xxx and speaks passionately about what he does and it sounds very interesting and the sort of thing that I very much want to be involved with. He has given me every encouragement and he is one of the reasons why I am here today.

19. What do you see yourself doing in the future?

Very few pupils leaving school, or even graduates, have a burning passion about their future – how can you when you have had so little experience of what the huge world of work has to offer? However, you are going to shoot yourself in the foot if you do not respond in some way related to the job that you are going for. It is quite acceptable at this stage of your life to be fairly general in your answer.

For example:

I would really like to work in the pharmaceutical industry because of its focus on health, but I'm not quite sure which job area to go for just yet.

I have always been fascinated by travel and different cultures, so I really want to explore career opportunities in the tourist industry and to find an area that I'm most suited to.

It is advisable to stay away from job titles unless you can handle the supplementary or follow-up questions that your answer might trigger. For example: 'So what do you think an Exhibition Events Client Manager actually does?' You are going to look really silly if you cannot answer with some pretty hard facts about the job you have mentioned and be able to say how you know the job in such detail.

On the other hand if you do know what job you would like, do find out as much as possible so that you can talk fluently about it. Better still, go and talk to some people who are already doing the job and find out not only what they do, but the challenges they face and what type of career it might lead to.

20. If you could be anyone in the world who would you want to be and why?

This is a silly question really but when we are young we do have heroes and this might give an interviewer an indication of either your role model or who you would like to be. If you mention anyone specific then be prepared for the inevitable supplementary 'Why?' You can choose someone outside the field you are going for and weave in some traits that would be well received in a corporate setting. For example, you could mention a famous footballer and then when you get the 'Why?' question you could give as a possible answer:

> Because not only is he very skilled but he is also a great team player and he never stops giving his best until the final whistle.

Any employer would want someone who aspires to being skilled, a good team player and giving of their best.

Questions for graduates

You are likely to get variations on the questions in the previous chapter but you will be expected to sound more structured, reasoned and fluent in your answers. Graduates pose the same selection conundrum to interviewers as school leavers. Since graduates usually have so little work experience to go on, inferences will have to be made from projecting your efforts at university into the work environment.

Questions asked could include:

1. Why did you choose to read your subject?
What is interesting here is did you make your choice because you enjoyed the subject, because you were good at it, because it had good career prospects, you thought it might be easy or because there was parental pressure to do what they did or fulfil an aspiration that your parents had for you? If it does not stretch the truth too much, the most appropriate answer is one with a career orientation such as:

> Ever since I played my first computer game I wanted to be in IT so the choice of degree was easy for me.

Should you answer in this way be prepared for some supplementary questions on what you like about the industry and the reason for your fascination.

2. If you are studying xxx why have you chosen not to pursue a career in xxx?

This is a testing question because there are obvious career paths for the likes of lawyers, engineers and even psychologists and what is not 'normal' sets off alarm bells in the ears of selectors. It may be the truth that after three years you can't stand the subject but it is unwise to admit it. It is not a major handicap since most managers and executives end up doing things they did not initially train for, but your answer must display some sort of logic if not rigor.

> I read law because it interested me and I knew that it would provide me with a strong disciplined approach to whatever career I decided upon. I found Commercial Law fascinating and that was the beginning of my interest in marketing. I am a creative person and integrating this with my formal academic training should provide a good basis for a career in marketing.

3. What have you done outside your studies?

This is where you can really score points especially if you have been elected to one of the offices of the society or if the society is directly related to the career path you have chosen. If you are in your first term of your third year and have spent the previous two years very sensibly chasing the opposite sex, going to rave parties and recovering from hangovers then may I suggest you join a couple of clubs or societies and attend just enough events for you to be able to talk about it with a vestige of credibility.

Rather like interests, your memberships can reveal much about you, your values and your motivation, so choose or disclose sensibly – extreme sports and bungee jumping, for example, are not usually associated with risk-adverse careers such as law or accountancy.

4. What did you do during your gap year?
Treat this as if you were making a report on a project outlining the reasons for your choice, the planning you undertook, your budgeting and financial planning and what you learnt or gained from the year. If you can tell some stories that have some relevance to or an implication for a future career so much the better. (I had everything stolen whilst in Morocco, I learnt to beg in French and Arabic, manage on nothing, have a great time and still get back to the UK via Spain and France without the help of Her Majesty's Government – it was interpreted as having flexibility, initiative and influencing skills as well as a gift for crisis management!)

5. Why did you choose this university?
Was it because of the status of the degree or the establishment itself, because you could live at home, because of a family tradition or because of the social life in the town?

Again, if you can, without stretching the truth too much, use the first reason, then this is the preferred option because of the career implications.

6. What do you know about us?
Do not, I repeat, do not attend an interview without doing your homework on the company – products/service, size, turnover, location, history and what makes them attractive as an employer. So do your

Internet search and your careers unit will probably have some recruitment literature and possibly even a set of the company's last year's accounts. However, be gentle with your interviewer because if you boast about all the research you have done, you will suddenly find that the tables have been turned on you and you will be grilled until your research is shown to be inadequate.

Everyone knows that the reason you have chosen this firm is because they pay well, have great promotion prospects and the possibility of international travel with all expenses paid, but you are going to find out as much as you can about their training. See if any of last year's graduates joined the organisation and network with them to get the inside story as well as the main issues and opportunities that the organisation currently faces. It is sensible to find out what a firm is really like before you join them, for an early mistake in your career can have implications for the next 40 years.

7. Why should we employ you?
This question is dealt with elsewhere in the book – see page 33 – but it is mentioned here because it is a very popular question with graduate recruiters who see anywhere between 80 and 120 graduates on the milk round. As advised, concentrate on your skills and competencies rather than the standard stuff that gets trundled out, such as: 'I am highly motivated, committed, hardworking, blah blah blah'.

8. What have you enjoyed most at university?
Whilst the question is structured to elicit a one-topic reply do not get caught out. Instead give three or four of your 'enjoyables' starting with the obvious ones.
  For example:

Well I have found my subject really interesting, especially xxx which I have enjoyed very much. The projects have been a challenge and, by and large, good fun; and, of course, being with and making friends with people who have similar interests to myself has made the social side great too.

9. What are your career aspirations?

Elsewhere in the book the advice is to side-step this question, but as a recent graduate you will be expected to have some well-thought-out career goals. You may want to be Executive Director Western Hemisphere but go easy on the ambition and keep your answer general rather than specific.

For example:

Well I would hope to have achieved a senior position in marketing within a reasonable timeframe either as a specialist or in a general management role, having had some exposure to sales and possibly PR along the way. I appreciate that success comes with both good performance and job opportunities. I certainly intend to work hard, learn as much as I can and make the most of every opportunity that comes my way.

10. Who else have you applied to?

No the answer is not 'None of your d**** business' because it provides you with an opportunity to convince the recruiter of your commitment to your career discipline and commercial or industrial sector. Just mention all their competitors.

For example:

Well I am definitely committed to a progressive career in marketing and I definitely want to join an organisation with strong and effective brand management. So I have also applied to Unilever and Procter & Gamble but the reason why I was interested in joining you was because . . .

Questions for women returners

The difficulty you will face here is not with the agency or with the HR department, who you will probably see for your first interview, but after you have been short-listed and go for your second interview. This is where you are likely to go one on one with the 'P' word – PREJUDICE. The market place is not only ageist and sexist, it is also risk adverse, so if you are a woman returner there are likely to be three hurdles for you to jump before you win that job offer. They are: younger candidates with more recent qualifications and experience.

Buy hey, don't give up now! Remember you would not have been short-listed by HR if you were thought to be unsuitable for the position. Your interviewers are just going to be a little more cautious over your application. Remember, if you can mange a home, a domestic budget and successfully negotiate with a two-year-old and still remain sane, you are probably experienced enough to manage a medium-sized company. For some strange reason most domestic experience is not valued by those who work – perhaps because work has traditionally been male dominated or perhaps this is just sheer ignorance of the myriad of skills, competencies and multitasking required to bring up children and manage a family.

You will definitely encounter interview questions to which you could answer: 'I will be happy to answer that question at the Industrial Tribunal because I am taking you there for discrimination!' Of course that is your choice but you are not likely to endear yourself to your potential employer. It is possible to ride over the discrimination positively as I hope to show below. I have marked the prejudicial questions with an asterisk(*).

1. **What brings you back into the workforce?**
    My children are now older, and having kept myself up to date in xxx with xxx training, and with my skills in xxx and xxx, I am looking forward to making a contribution in a commercial environment again.

2. **What made you give up work before?**
    My partner and I decided that we should have a family and that I should take responsibility for the rearing and early education of our children. It has been a wonderful experience not only being a mother but also learning to multitask. And having a three-year-old has certainly honed my negotiation and influencing skills. My time management has also improved ten-fold!

3. **In what ways do you think the industry has changed since you last worked?**
    From my reading, my training and keeping up with colleagues in the business, I know that today there is a greater emphasis on value through technical support brought about by increased competition – often global. Also the systems have probably changed, but, in my experience, technology makes things more

user friendly so I am confident that I will be able to get up to speed quickly.

4. **What do you think you will find most difficult should we take you on?**

I am not sure because I do not know the specifics of any recent changes. My confidence levels are high and I have kept my skills up to date. There could be some procedural issues in the way you would like things to be done, but I don't see that as being a difficulty – more a matter of learning and orientation.

5. **Have you ever been managed by someone younger than yourself?**

This may not be a concern for you, but for the young manager who might feel somewhat inadequate managing someone of more advanced years.

Yes, of course. Management is about skills and competencies rather than age, although age does bring its benefits. I suppose you are really asking would it be difficult for me to work for someone who is far younger than myself and I can assure you, having been taught xxx software by my son/daughter and his/her friends, this does not pose a problem for me in any way.

6. **What sort of people do you like to work with?**

People usually prefer to work with people like them-selves – it is not only birds that flock together – so this provides an opportunity for you to tell the interviewer about yourself in an indirect way. Think of the interviewer's ideal team and, providing it does not compromise you too much, say something like:

I like to work with people who are committed to their work, enjoy being part of a productive team and manage to have fun at the same time. I want to work with people who enjoy coming to work.

7. What arrangements have you made for the children?*

The children are at kindie/playschool now and arrangements to get them to and fro have been made and practiced. We have had a full discussion with the children so everything looks fine.

8. How do you think your children will react to you becoming a full-time employee again?*

As a family we discuss everything openly. For personal reasons I have spent some periods away from home and it has never been a problem. I think children are very resilient. I am confident that this will not be a problem.

9. What does you partner think about you returning to work?*

Of course we have discussed this thoroughly. We both agree that this is the right time to make the move back to work. I am still young enough to make a significant contribution and my skill set is still valid.

10. How computerate are you?

Very. I'm not sure how much this will be part of the job but I can use xxx and xxx. Usually, computing makes jobs easier not harder. I am not sure how this could be a difficulty.

11. What are you looking forward to most in returning to work?

Being part of a productive team, making a contribution, using my skills, enjoying the routine of work and getting my life into balance again.

12. How will you adjust to the routines after an absence of six years?

Having run, or should I say 'managed', a home for some time, the routines of work will come as a pleasant change. Routines are always helpful because you know where you are and can plan around them: in my experience work routines are more structured than those at home where you have to build in a great deal of flexibility.

13. What was it about the advert that prompted you to apply for this position?

Here you want to create a balance between what you want and what you can reasonably give to the company. As you can see from the suggested answer, the question does provide an opportunity to remind the interviewer of your skills as well as suggesting that you are offering a long-term commitment.

Well, in the advert, you were very clear about the skills required for the position – skills which I believe I possess. I am particularly confident in using xxx and xxx. In addition I could probably use my skills in xxx, and my experience in xxx will be an advantage. The job is interesting and, in the long-term, there may be some career opportunities. The company also enjoys a reputation as a good employer with reasonable job security, and as you can see from my CV I am not interested in job hopping.

14. How have you kept yourself up to date?

By and large, technology makes business systems smoother. Remember this is not a real issue for the interviewer: if it was a reservation about your ability to do the job, you would not have got the interview in the first place.

For an administrative position, then, something along the lines of:

> Home computing has ensured that I am up to speed on xxx and xxx and I am sure that advances in office equipment have made things easier rather than more difficult to use. I have also taken some evening classes in xxx so I am confident that I will fit in very quickly.

For a higher position, then, something along the lines of:

> In terms of computing skills, I have used the PC we have at home, and, for professional changes, I have done research using the information on the Net and journals. I have invested in a couple of programs on xxx. I have still kept up my professional memberships and I attend the meetings regularly, and then, of course, there is my network and we do lunches regularly.

15. What do you think this job involves?

Obviously I don't know the detail but essentially it is to achieve xxx through using xxx. Major challenges could include xxx and I will be working with xxx and my (internal/external) clients will be xxx.

16. How long have you been looking for a job?

This is difficult because you may have been looking for

ages and if you hint that you have been on the job market for an extended period the interviewer might think: 'There must be something wrong with this applicant that I have not discovered yet, otherwise he/she would have been snapped up.'

If this has been your experience then try something along the lines of:

> What is important is the type of job and the challenges it brings, so I have been very selective in my applications so far and this has taken time. At this stage of my career it is important that I accept the right job and the reason why this position is so attractive is because I have experience and skills in xxx and xxx and because of your reputation as an employer.

17. Do you see this as a job or as a re-launch of your career?

This is difficult. As a returner you are unlikely to be offered a traineeship and the job has become available because the employer has a specific need for work to be done. So if this is the case they are not going to want someone who is anxious to move on to meet their career aspirations as quickly as possible. On the other hand does an employer really want someone with no spark of aspiration at all? Perhaps a way around this conundrum would be to say yes and no at the same time.

For example:

> Well, I am very interested in this position because I am confident that I can make an immediate contribution and should there be a career opportunity further down the track then that would be interesting too.

18. Why do you want a full-time position?

Here the interviewer knows that your return to work is going to be a major change in your current lifestyle and the time structure in your life, so the risk here is: 'Have you thought through the implication of these changes?' Your answer should be consistent with answer 1 above:

> Because it is now the right time for me, given my present circumstances, and there is nothing that would get in the way of me giving my full commitment full-time. I have the full support of my family and there are no problems with the logistics on the hours required by the position.

The 'given my present circumstances' in your answer should ring a bell in the interviewer's head that he or she should not go there with a supplementary question because of discrimination legislation.

19. Won't this be a step down from what you did before?

The subtext of this question is initiated through a fear that you will get bored easily and then want to move on. You might want a quiet little number with no strain so that you can earn some money but still keep your life in balance. Obviously you are not going to share this reasoning with your prospective employer. Here you might wish to show that in offering you the position, the organisation is getting a bargain by saying something along the lines of:

> Yes that may be true but, as you can imagine, I have given this application a lot of thought and given my current situation and background I think it is right

that I take a position where I can do well immediately and use my skills and experience to our mutual advantage. There is great satisfaction in doing a job really well.

20. Describe you ideal working environment.
Since you do not know what the environment is in this particular organisation your answer has to be low on specifics and yet hint at the way you would approach the job. A bland answer such as the following might do the trick:

> I like working with competent people and, of course, in an environment which recognises contribution both from the individual and the team. Ideally I would like a position in a place where I enjoy coming to work.

ILLEGAL AND DISCRIMINATORY QUESTIONS

We all know that these are illegal questions but believe it or not somehow this information has not got through to a small number of interviewers. You have a choice – you can either answer them and stand a chance of getting a job or tell the interviewer that you are happy to answer the question at the Industrial Tribunal with the obvious job offer consequences. If you do go to a tribunal it is in your best interests not to mention this to other prospective employers.

Here are the naughty questions:

- Are you married?
- When do you plan to have children?

- Do you belong to a trade union/church/political party?
- How old are you?
- Where do you come from?

Psychologist questions

There are possibly three types of questions that a psychologist might ask. A psychologist is going to be interested in you as a person, the way you might cope with and approach your work and how you will fit into your work team and the culture of the company. You might be able to do the job, but if you do not fit in terms of your value it is unlikely that you will be successful. Also of interest will be the level of stress and role ambiguity you can work with and how you will respond under pressure.

You will see that I have also added the supplementary questions that would encourage you to provide more information about yourself. Many of the questions will be of the 'When did you stop beating your wife?' type, implying that at some time you have failed, worked with difficult people or been unhappy at work when none of these may be the case.

A word of warning/advice
It is sensible to answer these types of questions as honestly as you can. At interview it is relatively easy to present yourself for 40 minutes to an hour as being someone that you are not. What could occur is that your

act is recruited and not you the person. The job requires the latter – no one can keep up an act forever, but it is really easy to be yourself. If you present yourself as someone else, should you be offered the position you will be placing a great deal of stress upon yourself in addition to the rigors required by the new job. It does not matter how desperate you are for the position, your psychological health is far more important. Since your self-marketing and CV have already landed you one interview, you can be confident that you will soon gain another one. Things are not that desperate that you have to pretend to be somebody else.

1. Thinking back over your career, when were you most satisfied/happy?
This gives clues about what will satisfy you in a job. Also it will give an indication as to whether you have passed your career contribution peak. Research suggests that people are happy at work when they are learning and growing as a person because of the challenges in their work. What does it tell you when someone was happiest 15 years ago? It could indicate that they have been cruising in their job and they have come to you out of boredom from their present position rather than seeing it as a career move.

2. If you only had three adjectives to describe yourself what would they be? Please demonstrate each one from your career to date.
Obviously this is to check your self-perception and self-understanding. Think through your achievements and the themes that run through them and then distil the appropriate adjectives. In this way, not only will you come across as someone who is realistic but you will be well-prepared for the supplementary probe – 'Please give

me an actual example from your recent work of xxx'.

Your three words also have to match your behaviour during the selection process. I was once recruiting consultants for a London firm and a candidate, who was an Etonian, with very smooth and polished rapport skills, stated as one of his self-descriptor words that he was 'decisive' only later to take three times as long to answer a questionnaire as other candidates!

It would also be useful if you developed self-descriptors that had a direct bearing on the position that you are going for. It might be true, for example, that you are 'generous, thoughtful and artistic'. These are great attributes for someone to have, but unless you are going to be a philanthropist and set up an art centre for posterity, words such as 'creative, commercial and opportunistic' might push the balance in your favour if you were going for a job in sales.

3. Tell me about a time when you had to work with someone who you found difficult. What did you do?

It is pretty obvious what is wanted here, but it is difficult for interviewers to get this information in a subtle way without you knowing the real reason for the question. These days all of us are expected to have wonderful interpersonal skills, in spite of the fact that, to misquote Abraham Lincoln, 'you can't get on with all of the people all of the time'. You can still score some good points for yourself using the principles of the 'weakness' question – see page 78.

The general rule is to put anything negative or difficult as far back in your career as possible, so that it is not likely to be something that could affect your performance in the job on offer. So an answer could be something along the lines of the following. (You will see that it is quite an extensive answer and is in the form of a story – see page 35 for the benefits of stories. You will have to develop your own story for it to be credible:

> I get on with most people really, you have to. I can remember in my first job where, naturally, I wanted to do well and be successful but I must also have been a bit naïve, because it was a little while before I realised that one of the team members was pushing significant parts of her work my way. I had to do her tasks as well as my own. It was difficult for me being much younger and more inexperienced than her. Also not really knowing what I could and could not do in the situation. First I checked with other people in the team and discovered that she did this with all the new starts; then, without mentioning her directly, I checked with my manager. Having gained a clear picture of my role and hers I thought through how best to approach it.
>
> At first I thought that I would challenge her when she gave me some of her work, but on reflection I thought that this might be too confrontational. So instead I thought through the recent times she had given me work and just had a quiet word with her. I was very polite and took a 'I don't know' approach by saying something like: 'I am not sure about jobs xxx and xxx I am doing. I am thinking of going to Mike Smith (he was our manager then) and telling him about the difficulties I am having. The effect was fantastic, she took the jobs back and never asked me again!

4. What has been the greatest challenge in your career? Why was it a challenge for you?
Here is the basic rule: all achievements should be recent and confessed failures and mistakes, as we have said,

should be as far back in your career as possible. Recent achievements indicate that you are still learning, growing and developing: everyone makes mistakes when they are young and inexperienced.

But there is also an underlying danger in this question, because we only have challenges when we do not know how to do something. Babies are challenged trying to walk; we can do it without thinking. So be careful that the example you select does not indicate that you are a novice when it comes to a critical part of the position for which you are shooting.

So you have a choice: select something from your early career and show what you learnt from it or a recent achievement which you handled successfully, revealing skills and competencies that apply to the job on offer.

Again you will have to develop your own story but here is an example:

Because of technical advances in call-centre technology, I was keen for us to set up a centre in India which would save the company at least 35% in labour costs. I discussed it with my director and he set up the opportunity of doing a board presentation. I had presented before but not at board level and I was very passionate about getting their approval. First I got all the costs and ran them by the CFO. This ensured that it got his tentative approval. Then I approached the HR director because the plan might necessitate some redundancies. Now I had two directors on my side as well as my own.

I also discovered that one of our competitors had a similar set up to the one I was proposing and it was very successful. So I developed my presentation making it as short as possible. I then practiced and practiced my speech and developed some pretty good visuals. I also thought through how I would respond to negative challenges, should there be any. On the day, it went really well. Not only was the plan approved, but several of the directors subsequently congratulated me on my skills as a presenter. Obviously it helped me with my own director as well.

5. What has been your greatest disappointment in your career?

Here, the same advice as above is useful. Put the disappointment way back in the past – preferably in your first job and, not only confess your failing, show how you overcame it, what you learnt from the experience and confirm that it has not been a problem since.

For example:

Well, I am the sort of person that likes to get into the detail, but I can remember a time when, in my first job, I did so much research that I nearly missed the reporting date for the project and my boss thought that I managed my time poorly. That was a significant learning point for me, I still like the detail, but not at the expense of the required time constraints.

I have always been a very enthusiastic person and in my very first management position I can remember being very disappointed and concerned that I could not motivate a member of my staff. Fortunately an older manager, who was a mentor to me, suggested that this person was very introverted and my boundless enthusiasm would be, for him, a huge turn off.

The advice, which was spot on, was that I should tell the person what was required of him, give him the resources and authority to get on with it, and be more formal in my relations with him. It was a good lesson. I am still very enthusiastic but you have to adjust your style at times, in order to bring out the best in everyone.

6. What makes you think about leaving a job?

In other words, 'What are you demotivators?' We leave jobs for a host of reasons, including boredom, lack of challenge, poor pay or promotional prospects, relationship difficulties with co-workers or managers, disenchantment with the product or service, domestic and health reasons and many more. What the psychologist is attempting to do here, is to see if there is a correlation between what turned you off in your last job and the components in the job on offer. Should they be the same, or similar, there would be no point in making the offer since it is very likely that you would, in time, become demotivated and leave. There is no ideal answer here, it is perhaps best to be bland.

For example:

I have been doing my present job for x years and I am really on top of it, yet I feel more and more that I could make a greater contribution using my skills portfolio of xxx and xxx (these are, of course, the skills the new job demands). But this is not possible where I am, due to the structure of the organisation and the current management profile. One of the reasons that attracted me to this position was that my experience in xxx would ensure that I could make an immediate contribution. I must confess that a new environment is very attractive, as are, in the long-term, the improved career prospects.

7. If you had your career over again what would you do differently?

Another dangerous and sneaky question: why would we wish to change our successes? We'd want to change the occasions when we made an error of judgement or things went badly for us. As you have been advised before, wherever possible, put what you say in the distant past: say what you learnt from it and how you have since turned it to an advantage in the way you do things now.

Here is a suggestion based on the fact that very few people make the right career choice on leaving school or university:

> **Oh that is easy to answer, I would have gone into xxx (the area for the job on offer) straight from school/college and my career would have raced ahead.**

8. What sort of manager are you? Please give some examples.

The first part of this question is easy, the sting is where you have to give an example. Again, this is where the work on your achievement list is so helpful, because you work from what you have done back to a summary statement.

These days, managers are supposed to be team oriented, results driven, customer focused and be able to lead by example – a paragon of virtues.

If you think long and hard about your achievements, you will see where you have been able to demonstrate these wonderful qualities and consequently be able to answer along the lines of:

> **Well I am sure that if you asked my team, they would**

say that results are important to me and I expect all of us to make a contribution, because in the end we are going to stand or fall by what our customers think of us.

9. Describe your ideal subordinate.

This is an interesting question because what most people will do is, by describing their ideal, talk about themselves as a subordinate. So you have been warned.

Several surveys have suggested that the top two traits expected from employees are loyalty and commitment to their manager, product and organisation.

Capitalising on this information, your answer could be:

Ideally I would want someone who is committed to and enjoys their work and is loyal to the team and company as a whole. It is important to be proud of what you do. Being positive, I would like to work with positive people.

10. How do you work in a team? What contribution do you make? Please give me some examples.

Very few jobs these days do not require one to work in a team environment so you need a positive answer here. Also you need to think through what role you like to play in a team. Some people like to initiate projects, some like to control them, some like to evaluate them, some like to resource them and some like to complete them. (If you want to know more about this, read Belbin's work on teams). Thinking about the job on hand, it should not be too difficult to project yourself into the sort of team role which would be appropriate. A word of warning, though, if you really are a 'completer finisher' or a 'monitor evaluator' you will not do yourself any favours if you present yourself as something different because it is likely that you will not do so well in the job.

For example:

I have always worked in teams and enjoy the camaraderie and mutual support that teamwork provides. Recently, in the teams I've worked in, I usually end up making sure that the project keeps on track/is properly resourced/is completed on time, etc. For example, when I was with xxx I – [provide an example].

11. Tell me about a time when you showed initiative in a work situation. Tell me what you did specifically.

If you have done the achievements activity you will have lots of examples, but choose something which is directly relevant to the job you are going for, or demonstrates an essential competency. If possible, lead with the benefit to the organisation as a result of what you actually did and this will make your example more impressive and you more attractive.

12. What stresses you at work? How often does this occur?

Here do not be tempted to say 'nothing' for this will just blow your credibility. Nor will it help if you say 'people' because it could be interpreted that your interpersonal skills are not as strong as they could be. Coping with change falls into the same category, since we live in a corporate world of constant change we are supposed to be able to take this in our stride. A general non-committal safe answer is most appropriate.

For example:

I don't get stressed all that often, but a few years ago I can remember getting stressed when the project I ran was dependent on some resources which were totally outside my control. I know that you should not be concerned about things you cannot change, but it was important for the company and me personally to ensure that the project met the deadline. In the end it all turned out well but I had to pull in a lot of favours.

13. What sort of decisions at work are difficult for you to make?

As a manager you are paid to make decisions so this is rather like the stress question above. Of course, in your answer, it is best to avoid anything to do with your professional skills or the competencies required for the job.

For example:

When I have to make decisions that have a direct impact not only on the employee, but also on his or her family. Decisions like relocation, dismissal and redundancy are always hard to make. Perhaps another example would be to give a tough appraisal to someone who is already stressed in their job.

14. What do you think this job involves?

This is testing first, how much thought you have given to the job on hand and secondly, how much research you have undertaken. Both, of course, are equally important but the chances of you being able to spell out the exact KPIs required are minimal, so you need to cover yourself. Also, if you present a very firm answer and you are off the mark, the interviewer is going to have a thought bubble which says, 'This person is not going to do the job the way we want it done.' So you have another reason for being tentative. Notice in the example below that we have used the sale trick of assumptive language and also that we have attempted to get more information about the job from the interviewer.

For example:

I am sure that there will be specifics about the job that I will discover, but my experience suggests that some of the major requirements will be xxx and from the little I know about the company, there may be a special requirement for or an emphasis on xxx because of xxx. Naturally I am most interested in what the key criteria for success in the position are – could you outline them for me?'

15. What are you looking forward to most in this job?
This is easy. You are going to be employed to make a contribution or ease a current organisation pain. This question also provides an opportunity to remind the interviewer of your skills so a possible answer could be:

From what I know about the job, I am confident that I can make an immediate contribution in the area of xxx using my skills of xxx and xxx. I am also enthusiastic about taking up a new role.

If this sounds like you are delivering the career statement again you are right. But it is OK to repeat it. At interview you are in the self-promotion business and, like an advert on TV, if it is constructed well, it can be repeated.

16. How have you gone about fitting into a new environment?

This is a variation on the change question and is testing how you adjust to a new situation. A possible answer can be:

> Whenever I have changed job or been promoted in the past, I like to spend some time understanding the priorities, the people and the culture so that I can best position myself and my tasks. I feel it is a mistake to rush into things before you understand as much as you can about what is specifically required and the context of your work.

17. How does this job fit into your long-term career plans?

Again this is a dangerous question, for you want to appear reasonably ambitious but remember that you are being hired to do the job on offer and alarm bells will ring if it is your intention just to use the job as a spring board to the next stage of your career. Sometimes, even senior managers are reluctant to take on subordinates who could be a threat to their own career aspirations. So a little fudging would not be amiss here.

For example:

> I am the sort of person who likes to do the best I can. I am really interested in this position because of xxx and being a progressive company I am sure that there will be opportunities opening up for me. I really want a career which is satisfying, allows me to develop and provides a balanced lifestyle. I think this is more important than chasing a specific job title.

18. What has been the most difficult project or task you have had during your career?

This is the failure question which has been hidden in camouflage by a skilful questioner. 'Difficulty' is another way of saying, 'What did you lack in skills, knowledge or competence?' So the same rules apply: choose something not related to the job, put it in the past, outline briefly what you did and what you learnt from the experience.

Another approach could be to treat it the same as the difficult decision question and give a reply something along the lines suggested above.

19. What is the best way to manage you?

This is going to be fun to answer because most people like to do things one way and most companies like compliant employees who do it their way. It is a hypothetical question and there are so many variables – male/female boss, areas where you are/are not competent, you have/lack resources, how you are fighting time constraints etc. – that you can almost say whatever you want. In addition this question is likely to be asked by an HR interviewer so their likelihood of following up post-interview is minimal anyway. Here is a sample answer but it would be easy, given the above, to construct your own.

> I would like to think that once I got into the job and started hitting the KPIs satisfactorily, that I would need very little management. It is important for me to know what my priorities are and I like to have feedback on my performance, as well as coaching in those areas where I need to develop. I have had quite a few managers, all with very different styles in my time and I can't think of one with whom I did not get on well.

Standard line manager questions

Line managers are going to be more interested in what you have done and what you can do, than in you as a person. Usually you get to see your potential line manager as part of the second interview after the HR has screened out the 'unlikelys' and the 'improbables'. The really good news here is that you are already thought to have what it takes to do the job – otherwise you would not have been short-listed – your task now is that you have to convince the interviewer that of the five or so people to be seen you are the ideal candidate.

At this stage you should, from your first interview, your research and the original advertisement, have a very clear idea about what is really required in the job, in terms of skills and competencies. Having done the suggested activity on your achievements (see pages 31–32) you can now prepare by correlating all those achievements with what you know about the job on offer.

1. Tell me about your experience in this sort of work?
This will be the main thrust of the line manager's questioning since their main concern will be around super question number one: 'Can you do the job?'

Your answer should weave around your career statement and of course be based on what you have been able to find out about the job. Since you do not know at this stage what the priorities are for your potential line manager, you can also use this reply to lay out a list of your skills in the hope that in the supplementary questions, the manager will invite you to enlarge on one of them. As you will see in the suggested answer you might even take the opportunity to gain more information.

A suggested framework for an answer could be:

I have been in this business for xxx years now and have gained a number of skills including xxx, xxx, xxx and xxx through my experience in xxx, xxx and xxx. Is there a particular emphasis which this position has or is there a particular opportunity that needs to be addressed at this time?

2. When in your career did you first have responsibility for others?

Even if you do not get this question directly and the position has some management component, you will need to get this information across. Not only do you have to say when, but it would also be useful to give an indication of numbers, especially if you have had control of five or more people.

Management jobs wax and wane with the number of direct reports. So, in your reply, talk about the largest number that you have ever had reporting to you, using a phrase such as 'up to'. Also, if you have managed through others, talk about the total headcount for which you were responsible and not just your immediate direct reports. If this is some time ago, do not mention how long ago. You will see in the example how you might try and encourage the interviewer to ask supplementary questions in a different area (in the example this is 'challenges'), thus avoiding the interviewer asking 'When was that?'

Even if you are going for a supervisory job, talk about managing people rather than supervising them; it sounds far better since management implies so much more.

For example:

> I first had responsibility for people back in xxx and since then have managed many teams with a total responsibility for up to xxx. I enjoy getting things done in a team environment even more so when there is a challenge in the work which gets us all pulling together.

3. How long will you stay in this job? What are you long-term career aspirations?

Both of these questions are essentially the same. There is a job that needs to be done and the manager wants someone to fill it and not be away as soon as possible or indeed be a threat to their own position. It is best really to duck the question with a general response such as:

> As long as I can make a contribution. Every new position presents a challenge and I am looking forward to such an opportunity. As the position grows, because all jobs change, I am sure there will be future challenges. Also, being a progressive company there might be opportunities for me in the future.

4. How would you describe you management style? Give me some examples.

Here you have at least three choices:

- Tell the absolute and whole truth – not advised because no one is perfect
- Take a punt at what you think the style of the manager is and reflect it back – not advised unless you are absolutely sure of yourself
- Give the 'flavour of the month' management answer – recommended

Something like this might get you off the hook:

My colleagues have always said that I have a participative style for most of the time, especially when we are agreeing methods and allocation of resources. In the past I have become assertive when the situation demands it or I think someone is not pulling their weight when they should. I think it is very important to treat everyone with respect and even more important to recognise and say thank you for work well done or for extra effort given.

Questions for salespeople

Here you will find some technical questions relating to your selling experience. Because everyone's experience is unique, it will not be possible to suggest suitable answers in every case. To assist you for each question, there are some strategies and tips with which you can work so you can develop your own powerful answers.

Questions 10 to 13 in this section are obviously about your technical skills as a salesperson. It is important that each story you tell has a positive and successful outcome. If you have completed the achievements activity and have them BSTARed as suggested on pages 34–35 you will find these questions easy to answer.

Where possible, use different sales stories to answer the questions. It could be that one sales war story would cover them all but much better to select from a large quiver of war stories where you were successful.

Recent experiences will be more powerful than those in the distant past because it will show that you are still on the ball.

1. When did you first earn money independently from your family?
This is a very powerful question because it indicates a

whole host of sales attributes, including: a need for independence, personal responsibility, an understanding that money is important and realising what money can do. It also shows your influencing skills since you had to convince someone to employ you. Interestingly enough, most top salespeople and successful self-made entrepreneurs started earning before they were ten years old.

You can't tell fibs here but the advice is, the earlier you started making money independently of your family, the better. Do not forget to weave into your answer how you persuaded someone to give you a job.

2. What sports did/do you play/were you interested in when you were young/now?

This obviously is getting at your team orientation and your level of competitiveness. You can read far too much psycho-babble into this stuff, but, by and large, someone who concentrates on individual sports is more likely to respond well to individual bonus systems. Sport at a high level can also indicate a fair level of self-discipline and self-determination.

Obviously you do not have to be good or keen at sport to be good at sales but it is an acceptable outlet for strong competitive traits when young.

Some sports, such as golf, provide wonderful business networking opportunities as do memberships of clubs such as sailing organisations.

If you claim to be interested in a sport, make sure that you can handle the supplementary questions – many a time I have seen an interest in squash or swimming mentioned on a CV only to discover at interview that the person has not been near a court or the pool in ages.

3. What took you into sales in the first place?

Here is an opportunity for you to get across aspects of

your personality that underpin sales competencies and skills. Not all sales recruiters are going to ask you questions about your disposition, but will make inferences from what you say about your work experience. This question allows you to talk about your personality which is far superior to having it inferred.

For example:

> I suppose I have always had the ability to persuade and influence people, which has been useful throughout my career. Also, it is very rare that you are the only person the buyer is talking to, so there is always an element of competition and it is great when you win the sale against others who may be as good or even better than you.

4. What do you like best about sales?

Sales could be attractive for a whole host of reasons, so here we have fudged the answer to get across something about you which makes you a natural at sales:

> In sales you meet all sorts of people who need to be approached in different ways. I like the challenge of meeting people and developing strategies to work with them.
>
> Sales is perhaps the one area in business where you get definite and very fast feedback: you either make the sale or you don't. If you don't there is always the opportunity for feedback as to why, and this is a learning opportunity for you to get better. I also get a buzz when I have solved a problem for a client/customer and satisfied their need.

5. What do you like least about sales?

A dangerous question because it is almost the same as

the 'What are your weaknesses?' question. On the other hand, you are not likely to come across as the most honest person in the world if you say, 'I love it all'. If you can, either avoid the question altogether or choose one of those aspects of the job which are not that significant.

For example:

> When I started out in sales, I found that, at times, the paperwork could be a little tedious, but you soon learn that it just has to be done. On some contracts, I find it a little frustrating when you are invited to make a pitch just so the firm can say that it went out to tender, but in reality it had already identified their preferred supplier. Sometimes, too, even after you have qualified the prospect, you find that the person pretends that they have the buying authority, but in fact they have to refer up – this I find testing because you have to start all over again.

6. What do you know about our product/service?

At any job interview you will be expected to have done your research and found out as much about the product as possible – would you take on a salesperson who did not bother to go to this amount of effort? However, there is also a difficulty here. You will not know as much as the interviewer, so if you flaunt your knowledge, your potential manager will test you to destruction. This being the case, it is important to preface all your research with some humility.

For example:

> Well, I do not know as much as I would like, but I have looked you up on the Net, reviewed the product brochure and gone through your last set of accounts, so the main points that come through are: . . . [here

you tell the interviewer all that you know]. But I would be interested to hear how you feel the product/service sits in the market and what you see as the main opportunities given the current state of the market.

The professional interviewer will be as brief as possible in their answer, but it would be hard for a sales manager or director to not wax lyrical about the products and services of the company. Here you listen and relate what is being said to your experience and achievements. When it is your turn to speak you can say:

It was interesting that you mentioned xxx because when I was with the xxx organisation I . . . [and you then go on to share your related achievements].

7. Who has had the most influence on you in your career in sales?

Here you can choose anyone you like as long as they were or are in sales. However, be prepared for the supplementary questions 'Why?' and 'How were you influenced?' The other alternative is to mention sales gurus such as Zig Ziglar or Tom Hopkins. You could even mention a popular guru such as Charles Handy or Tom Peters, but in all cases you must be ready to show what you learned from their seminars and/or their books. If there is a sales system that you feel is appropriate for the job you are going for, such as Neal Rackham's SPIN selling, then you could use this.

In any case, it is useful if the area in which you were influenced is directly related, in some way, to the position on offer or the product or service you will be selling.

8. What have you done to develop your skills over the last 12 months?

No job ever stays the same, and in management there are always the latest fashions usually being purveyed by American authors and consultants. It is important to show that you are still growing and developing as a sales professional. You can mention the books you have read or the seminars you have attended unless of course you are studying, but do not leave it there. Show how you have applied this knowledge to your work.

9. Take me through your typical sales cycle.

Think of your most difficult sales success in the recent past and tell the story from the beginning, right through to closing the deal. As we already know, stories are far more powerful than giving textbook answers. Because it is your story, it will be easier for you to justify any challenges from a technical point of view, such as: 'Why didn't you attempt a trial close earlier?'

10 Tell me how you qualify a prospect from your actual experience.

For example:

> This is very important because you can waste a lot of selling time to the wrong person. It is not always easy because you do not want to upset the prospect or damage the relationship. In fact that is where I start – it does not matter whether or not the person I am talking to is qualified and has the authority to buy. I will still need their support in the process, so I hold back on qualifying until I have developed a rapport and a trusting relationship with the person.
>
> When I am confident that I have the trust of that person, I feel ready to ask gently, with a polite

preface, 'I hope you don't mind me asking, but before I work on the tender/proposal, I am right in thinking that you have the authority to purchase providing we can satisfy your needs and come to an agreement on price?' I think it also helps in that it shows the prospect you are working with that you are a professional and have significant calls on your time.

11. What is the most difficult selling situation you have ever faced?

Most salespeople agree that it is difficult to close a deal when your competition is significantly cheaper and offers comparable or better quality and service. Again, if you have a suitable story, here is the place it can be delivered.

12. What is the most successful sales close you have ever made?

Again this is an opportunity for a story rather than a textbook answer. You can weave the theory stuff into your answer mentioning the 'time close' or the 'walk away close' but stories get remembered far more easily than the dry facts of theory. It also makes you sound more credible.

13. Tell me about the most difficult client/customer you have ever had.

Here you need to show that you were dealing with the customer from hell, rather than you lacked the rapport and interpersonal skills to win the prospect over. Personally it is a big call to be able to get on with absolutely everyone, but in sales you are expected to be able to get on with everyone professionally. It would also be useful, as well as safe, if you chose a customer profile or an environment you are unlikely to encounter in the job on offer.

If you are stumped for an example then customers who are economic with the truth are a safe bet for a story.

As with all your sales stories be ready for the supplementary questions such as: 'And what did you do?' or 'And what was the outcome?'

14. Tell me about a time when your competitor's price was lower than yours.

This is the classic interview question for salespeople that almost always gets asked. Again recall your achievement list and BSTAR the story.

15. What sort of person do you find it easy to sell to?

People usually get on well with others like them, and when this happens the selling process just flows so easily even when there are price and quality or delivery issues. But you might like to try a different tack and talk about selling to professional buyers who know what they want and know how to negotiate since this will place you in a more professional light.

16. What sort of person do you find it difficult to sell to?

This is a variation on question 13 above and the comments there apply here as well.

17. Tell me about a presentation you have made?

This is a real BSTAR opportunity for you. If possible, make it a presentation that you made to some heavy rollers, either inside or outside the company, and on a topic or service related to the job you are going for.

This question also provides you with an opportunity

to show how good you are with the latest audio-visual technology.

18. Tell me about a time when you had to let a client/customer down.
This is bad news so follow the basic rule and put this event a long way back in the past. Also, don't take personal blame for the misfortune – sales are usually let down by either production or by logistics.

For example:

> Fortunately this has not happened recently but about x years ago I made a sale, rang back to Production Control who assured me they could meet the customer's delivery requirements. You can guess what happened – when I got back to the plant, I just happened to talk to the production manager about my sale and he did the proverbial 'You want it when?!' When your back is to the wall, I have always found it useful to tell the truth and be first with the bad news. Rather than ring the customer, I went to see him as soon as possible and explained the situation and why. Fortunately he was able to amend his schedules accordingly. He also appreciated both my initiative and my integrity, which came in useful when a competitor attempted to steal this customer. It was a good early lesson to learn. Even now I don't agree delivery dates until I have checked personally with those who can deliver.

19. What is it about you that you think makes you successful?
This question is a variant on, 'Why should I select you as opposed to anyone else on the short list?' Just as products have Unique Selling Points (USPs) so do you.

Treat yourself as a product and remember that everyone the interviewer is seeing is already thought able to do the job. In seeing all the candidates the interviewer is continually asking, 'Who is the best here?' This being the case you really must think through what it is in your experience that makes you special and a cut above the others in the short list. Similar industry, similar customer demography, similar product base are the things to concentrate on where you can. (See page 33.)

20. What sort of support do you need from the organisation?

If you say 'nothing', you are in danger of appearing arrogant; if you ask for too much you are in danger of being thought a problem before you even start. To get off the hook of this conundrum just request what would be normal in any company induction including:

- Product orientation and familiarisation
- Client lists and customer profiles
- Sales administration processes
- Outline of the technological support you will get

Or use a bland response.
For example:

> You have been most helpful in outlining the position and I am confident that I will settle quickly and be able to make an effective contribution, but I will need to familiarise myself with your major customers and their profiles so that I can get up to speed quickly. I also need to know what sort of technological support I can expect and there may be some software training but I am pretty computerate, so that should not be a difficulty.

21. Sell this pen/computer/office space/mobile phone to me.

This was a question you could almost guarantee getting in the 1980s and it is still a favourite with the outgoing, assertive and action orientated sales manager. There is no problem here, just go through your normal sales process showing off some techniques.

> Mr Hutton, thank for your time and I know you are busy but I am confident that what I have to show you today will impress you and you are a person who is not easily impressed. What is the thing that annoys you most about your phone? . . . Yes and you're not the only one. That is why this phone has overcome those annoying problems by xxx.
>
> Not only that, Mr Hutton, but this phone will also give you the additional benefits in that it will give you xxx, so that you can xxx and when you make or receive calls you will be amazed at the reception clarity.
>
> Naturally you would think, Mr Hutton, that a new state of the art instrument such as this would be expensive, but you will be impressed to know that your investment in the rental is no more that your current provider. In fact if you sign today for a 12-month period, I can even give you a 10% discount. Now, Mr Hutton, which do you think you would prefer? The black, the titanium or the blue? . . . Good choice, now shall I make the invoice out to you or the company?

So here you have used the prospect's name four times, discovered his needs by listening, customised your benefit presentation to those specific needs, used assumptive language, dealt with price, made a time and a discount trial close, given a triplicate of choice and topped off all this with the classic alternative close. Not bad for only three paragraphs!

Phrases that sink you

Now we know that interviewers, like most accountants and lawyers, are risk adverse, so you have to be careful about how you present information about yourself. Sometimes a modest phrase can be like a modest iceberg to the *Titanic*. Here are some examples:

I ENJOY A CHALLENGE

Oh really? Doesn't everyone? Is any candidate who does not, likely to be taken on? The phrase also implies that you cannot do something. We are challenged by what we cannot do or have not done. When we have the skills and experience, we are not likely to be challenged. Most interviewers would be very rich if they had a pound for every time during an interview they heard the phase, 'I enjoy a challenge'.

TO BE HONEST . . .

Now this innocent and very common phrase is often said in good faith, but the inference is that everything you have said before is not quite the truth. Usually the phrase is used in self-defence. For instance, when you are asked a direct question about a skill or some aspect of your experience and you don't have it.

Compare the responses to this question:

Have you used the Tracker software to manage your sales base?

Response 1:

Well, to be honest, no but I have used something called Maximizer.

Response 2:

Tracker is very similar to Maximizer: a database management system of which I have a great deal of experience, so my confidence in mastering Tracker is high. The trick is not so much knowledge of the software but how to get maximum results from it.

Both answers are honest but the latter is a far stronger response. Also, whilst both responses imply a learning need – a negative for the employer – in the second response this negative is hidden in the middle and consequently softened.

I AM KEEN TO LEARN / I PICK THINGS UP QUICKLY . . .

This is like hanging a huge notice round you neck in flashing neon lights broadcasting in capital letters 'PLEASE TRAIN ME'. Employers are not in the business of training employees, but getting them to produce at their maximum. Training is a cost. Given two candidates, one who indicates that he will need training and the other who needs training but says nothing, it is obvious which one will get the job offer.

If you do have to admit that you will need training, then slip this into the middle of your response (as in the example immediately above).

I AM GOOD WITH / I LIKE PEOPLE / I LIKE HELPING . . .

For those jobs with a high service component you frequently get questions on how you got into this line of work or what you like about it and this is the classic naff response.

Try this in response to the question:

How did you get into this line of work?

Well, to a certain extent sales is about needs: a person's or an organisation's needs, and when I have been involved in that process I gain a great deal of satisfaction.

This is like saying, 'I like helping people' but is a much stronger response. When I was a full-time graduate recruiter, I vowed that I would never take on someone who wanted to go into HR because 'they liked people'.

In these service oriented jobs, liking people goes with the territory and is taken as read. Even if you are the most out going, friendliest person in the world, please do not use this fatuous phrase.

I AM A GOOD WORKER / I WORK HARD / I GET THINGS DONE / I AM A HIGH ACHIEVER

Of course you are and of course you do, but this is automatically assumed. Anybody who wants a job is going to present themselves as someone who will perform well. To say this smacks of desperation, and desperate candidates only get offers from desperate employers.

AS I SAID BEFORE / AS IT SAYS ON MY CV

This is just a slap in the face for the interviewer and is French for, 'Did you not listen to what I said?' or 'Have you not read my CV thoroughly?' Sometimes the interviewer will be like a barrister in cross-examination going back to a topic again and again to see if the answer is consistent or if it changes slightly. Sometimes it is because the interviewer had covered the topic earlier but forgotten to ask you a supplementary on a particular point.

PUFF LANGUAGE

If you have to use it, keep puff language for your resume and covering letter and not for the interview. Avoid sexing up your experience with phrases such as:

- I am excellent at . . .
- I have vast experience in . . .
- I have superior skills in . . .
- I am brilliant at . . .

If you really are good at something then preface your ability with a softening phrase.

Here are some examples:

- People say that I . . .
- My boss complimented me on . . .
- My last appraisal stated that I . . .
- Somehow I have developed a reputation for . . .
- I am known in my team for . . .
- My colleagues have always said . . .

These phrases take the edge off what could otherwise be seen as your egomania, but the advice is: use them frugally during your interviews.

TENTATIVE LANGUAGE

Now here is the reverse of puff language. Sometimes, even without knowing it we give ourselves away or hint that we are not confident in our abilities. We do this through the use of tentative language – little phrases such as 'I think . . . / I feel . . . / I believe . . . / I hope . . .' All of these phrases will soften and dilute the impact of what you say.

For example:

I think I would enjoy that aspect of the job.

contrasted with

I would enjoy that aspect of the job.

I feel confident that I would develop new sales.

contrasted with

I am confident that I would develop more sales.

So perhaps you might feel able to try and leave your tentative language outside the interviewer's door – maybe!

Thinking time and those 'Ums' and 'Ahs'

Nearly as bad as tentative language is the 'ums' and 'ahs' we utter whilst we are thinking. This is a very natural process, although some of us engage in it more than others. Sometimes we worry that if we spend time thinking about the best way to answer, it might be interpreted as stupidity or being a bit slow. Not so! But if this thinking time worries you, then you can use what are called process statements. These contain no information but they let the interviewer in on the thought processes going on in your head. It happens all the time on radio where silence is forbidden. Here's an example:

Q: Why did you leave that job?
A: Er . . . (10-second silence) . . . Um, it was a good career move and I must confess that the increase in salary was particularly welcome at that time.

With process statements:

Q: Why did you leave that job?
A: Let me see . . . that was five years ago . . . and at that time . . . we had just had our first baby . . . A friend, who I had previously worked with rang and offered

146

me a job because of my experience with UNIX. It was a good career move and I must confess that the increase in salary was particularly welcome at that time.

All that you have done here is let the interviewer in on the thought processes which are going on in your head.

Popular interview questions

Now we cannot guarantee that you will get all, some or none of these questions but they probably cover about 80% of the question areas that you will be challenged on outside your area of technical expertise. To prepare questions about your technical skills and experience, just ask yourself: 'If I was recruiting for this position what questions would I ask to reassure myself that they could do the job?'

Where possible, provide an answer where you can top or tail your response with a specific example from your career history. A good interviewer will get this by asking supplementary questions, but you will soon discover that there are very few good interviewers out there even amongst HR professionals. If you only provide general answers, you will leave the interviewer with a warm and comfortable feeling about you, but no good solid reasons for taking you on. Also if this is your first interview and the interviewer has to justify to a line manager why you should be seen, he will be hard-stretched to come up with some good reasons.

Since most interviewers have not been trained, the majority of the following questions are formatted as 'Open questions' (see page 45). Once you have mastered answering them you might like to be more rigorous with yourself and convert them into 'Behavioural questions' (see page 45).

For example:

What decisions do you find difficult to make?

Could be changed to:

Tell me about a time when you had to make a decision that you found difficult. Please be specific.

Remember that the example answers are just that. They give you the flavour of an answer or an approach, but you must do the work, having done your achievement list, of making them your own with your own examples.

1. **Why do you want this job? What attracted you to this job?**
   This position offers me the opportunity to use and develop my skills particularly in xxx as well as being able to make a significant contribution in an area which I enjoy.

   This job interests me because it offers greater variety than I have in my present position. I will also be able to develop my skills in xxx.

   I am attracted to this position because I want to be able to make more of a contribution through what I do, and it is the logical next step in my career having spent significant time doing xxx.

2. **What do you consider yourself good at doing?**
   Completing tasks on time, for example . . .

Working under pressure / tight deadlines, for example . . .

Prioritising my work and being able to multitask effectively, for example . . .

3. What sort of person are you at work?
Easily approachable and helpful especially when people are having difficulties.

I have always been positive in my approach to work. To me challenges are opportunities to learn and develop, as well as having the satisfaction of getting the work done. My biggest challenge was . . .

Highly team oriented. I enjoy working with others and giving my best within a team environment, whether it be with my colleagues or with the people for whom I am responsible. In teams you can get more done, more effectively and more cheaply whilst having fun at the same time.

4. How long did it take you to settle into your present job?
I usually adapt myself quite quickly because of my experience in . . . Every organisation has different ways of doing things and different procedures, but it is rather like computer software: once you are up to speed in one system it is easy to adapt to another. In any job it is important to make a significant contribution as quickly as possible.

5. How do you like to get things done at work?
Planning has always played an important part in the way that I like to approach work. Once I know the

specific outcomes required and thought through the best way to achieve them, I find that the work just flows and gets done effectively. For example . . .

Given a choice I will first do the things I like the least, and then the tasks which follow are always more enjoyable. Therefore my work days always get better.

The first thing I do in the morning is revise my 'to do' list and set the priorities for the day based on what is urgent and where I can make the best use of resources. In this way, I always know what I should be doing next and those things which do not get done are usually not essential or significant.

6. In what environment do you work best?
   A challenging environment where I can put my skills to the test, be part of a team, and gain recognition for work well done.

   In an environment where supervision is minimal but leadership and guidance are readily available.

   A fast-paced environment which provides an opportunity to multitask, test my abilities and which stimulates me to perform at my optimum.

7. How did you change the job you have been doing?
   I helped create a more friendly and co-operative atmosphere in my department, which fostered team spirit and decreased absenteeism, subsequently productivity dramatically increased.

   I was innovative in that I redesigned and introduced xxx and by doing so, the results were . . .

We had a problem with xxx and I suggested that we do xxx which was accepted and as a result . . .

8. What motivates you? What excites you at work?
    I enjoy working with innovative and competent people who value hard work and like to get things done effectively.

    Seeing the results of my work and knowing that I have contributed to the overall success of the department/company.

    An harmonious environment with friendly colleagues.

    A whole host of things, really, depending on the situation. In the past. I have been motivated by:

    • The job
    • The opportunity to be creative
    • Achieving an almost impossible objective
    • Helping the team give of their best

9. If you could change your job in any way, how would you do it?
    Decrease the repetitive tasks.

    Increase the scope of my responsibilities so I can challenge myself, develop new skills and make a more significant contribution.

    Streamline some of the processes so that the overall procedure is more efficient and so free up more time to . . .

10. How have you changed over the last five years?
I have definitely got better at xxx as well as improving my skills in xxx because of my experience in xxx.

I have gained more direction and a better perspective of where I am going and what I want to achieve. I am far more focused on what I do.

I have gained more confidence as a xxx through my exposure to xxx. This confidence has spilled over to other areas of my work including xxx.

11. Describe a time when you felt that you were doing well.
This question provides you with an opportunity to highlight one of your USPs (see page 33). Remember to make sure that your answer is FABed (see pages 31–32) and if you can, tell a story with a BSTAR structure (see page 34).

12. What would your colleagues say about you?
I am a very easy person to get along with and my ability to xxx is good.

They would probably say that I am hardworking and proficient. I have a reputation for setting goals with a certain amount of stretch in them and I can display great focus when it is necessary.

13. Describe a situation that was difficult for you and what you did about it.
In the past when I encountered a difficult situation, I have spent time reviewing the problem and the factors that have brought it about. Then I develop as

PERFECT ANSWERS TO INTERVIEW QUESTIONS

many options as I can, and once I've thought through all the probable outcomes, the way forward is pretty clear. For example . . .

I once had to complete a project under tight team pressure with very limited resources. The situation was . . . [tell a BSTAR story] . . . The key really was for me to become more flexible and do some extra overtime for a short period.

14. Who are you finding it difficult to work with right now?

At present I am not finding it difficult to work with anyone. Some time ago, I did have difficulty with a colleague who was not pulling his weight and as a consequence our work was falling behind time. After some straight talking it seemed to work out OK, although he did leave three months later.

Rarely do I find it difficult to work with people and I certainly get on very well with my present team. I have always found that if you respect others, they usually warm to you and a working relationship develops.

15. Why did you leave that job/Why do you want to leave your current job?

I felt that I was not using my professional skills and knowledge and I was beginning to get bored, as well as frustrated, knowing that I could do better.

The stability of the company was questionable and I need to work somewhere where there is a reasonable degree of job security.

I had gone as far as I could, my manager was only three years older than myself and so I was looking down the barrel of doing the same job for a number of years to come.

Personal reasons really. Now that I have a family, the daily travel to and from work is just too long and my life is out of balance. I will be sorry to leave because I enjoy my work but getting there and back is just too much.

16. Why did you stay with that organisation for such a short time?

The job I was given was not what was outlined in the recruitment literature or during the interview, and I felt let down. Since then I have always done better research before accepting a position.

Because of a restructure soon after I joined, which I was not told about at interview, the job I accepted changed out of all recognition. My main skills are in xxx and that is what I want(ed) to concentrate on.

The autocratic sexist management style of my boss was totally unacceptable – in fact I lasted longer than the two previous job holders.

The company has a new CEO and the values of the organisation changed considerably as well as its ethics. It was not the company I joined, nor the sort of place with which I want to be associated.

17. Why did you stay so long in that organisation?

Well, in fact, whilst there I had three promotions and

one transfer so it was rather like having four different jobs.

I stayed because the job was continually challenging. Whilst the job title stayed the same, the technology was always changing, so it was like having several different jobs.

Most of my work was involved with one project after another – each project usually bigger and more demanding than the previous one – and so it never felt like being in the same job because it was always changing.

18. Why were you/have you been out of work so long?
If you have been out of work for more than two months, potential employers naturally ask themselves why this is, and why another employer hasn't made you an offer: asking themselves is there something about this candidate I have missed? The more senior and/or better rewarded the job, the more difficult and thus longer it takes to secure them, because of the competition. Remember the length of time is not a major problem, otherwise you would not have been seen, but you have to give a reasonable and credible answer.

At that point in my career it was important to take some time out, consider my options and decide the direction I wanted to travel in my career. It was a very useful time, if somewhat self-indulgent, but it was time well spent and if I had not done it I would not be here today.

To be successful in xxx I knew that I had to develop my computing skills and experience, especially in the area of xxx. I was not in paid work but I was/have been working very hard at xxx and now have so much more to offer as an employee.

I am not looking for just a job but a career and consequently I have been very selective in who I have approached for a position. I came to you because you have a reputation for xxx.

19. Why were you made redundant/let go?

What is important here is not to bad mouth your firm even if after 20 years of hard work they treated you abominably. People do not sell more Pepsi by rubbishing Coca-Cola. If you get emotional and start talking about 'giving them the best years of your life', etc., you will spiral down, get it off your chest and NOT get the job offer.

Here is a process for you:

1. Forge a link to what the interviewer probably knows about or has heard about.
2. Talk about the restructure in a rational way – even better if you can comment on how sensible it was and how you would have done the same in a similar situation.
3. Say that you were one of a 'cast of many' (if more than 50 people give the figure because it adds weight to the argument that your demise was just business and not personal).
4. State what a good opportunity it was for you to review where you are in your career and that you've now decided you are ready and committed to move on.

Here is a possible answer that you can tailor to your

own position and circumstances. This is one of those answers that you really should practice saying out loud to yourself so that, should this question be asked, you are confident, positive, credible and ready for your next career challenge.

> As you have probably read in the press, the tele-communications industry is continually downsizing and restructuring itself in the face of global competition. My unit has escaped several restructures – which came with such regularity we called them autumn manoeuvres. It became our turn and the reshuffle was very sensible; I would have done it slightly differently but it really had to be done. About 75 of us were affected altogether and my position became redundant and I was let go. Unfortunate, but a fact of life these days. However, the good thing is that it was about time I moved. I've been able to do a lot of work on reviewing my strengths and skills profile, as well as what I want to do. That is why I am here today, because I am definitely committed to gaining a position in xxx.

20. On a scale of one to ten with ten being the highest, how important is your work to you? Why not a ten?

> Fairly high, perhaps a seven or eight. You are what you do and you spend more time at work than you do in any other activity, but, on the other hand, it is important to have balance in your life as well as other interests. My family and friends play a big part in my life, so the trick is to make a life which is in balance and harmony with all the major components.

21. If you did not have to work what would you do?
This question is dangerous because your response indicates your true priorities. Saying that perhaps you would do the same sort of work but in a charity environment would be ideal because it would indicate how committed to your work you are.

Obviously the point to get across is not that you would just chill out on a beach in Nirvana somewhere, but continue to use your skills and develop yourself as much as possible.

For example:

See more of my family and friends but I would have to work, because I enjoy what I do and I am the sort of person that needs to continually develop and grow. Perhaps I would see if I could work part-time and put myself on some courses.

22. What decisions do you find hard to make?
Difficult decisions are usually challenges: when you get them right it is great, when you get them wrong they provide a learning opportunity. I usually have difficulty when there is a conflict between heart and head, for example . . .

I find it difficult to make decisions when I do not have all the facts that are necessary to make the right decision, and I have to take a punt. My style is that I would rather be right first time, even if it takes a little longer, than making a quick decision and then having to spend even more time putting it right.

The most difficult decisions I have to make are when it has a direct effect on people's lives or could have huge implications for the future of the company.

23. What decisions do you find easy to make?

Those decisions where the correct answer is mainly to do with reason and logic. I enjoy making decisions that call upon my experience and skills, for example . . .

24. What do you think are the major challenges and opportunities facing this organisation?

For obvious reasons it is not possible to illustrate a possible answer here but it is a question that you might expect, especially if you are in the running for a senior position.

All organisations face difficulties with competition, technology and developments in products or services and this is where your networking would prove invaluable. Your Internet search and reading of the business pages should also help you here. Remember that since organisations operate in a market place, it is likely that firms in the same sector will be facing the same types of difficulties.

25. Have you bought our product/used our services?

Now obviously this will not apply if you are going for a job with British Aerospace or HMS Prison Service but where possible you should be able to talk constructively and credibly on the subject that is obviously dear to the interviewer's heart. With FMCGs it is almost essential that you can talk about brands and models. As a consultant I nearly lost an assignment with Goodyear in Wolverhampton since my car was running on French Tyres. It was the same when, as a young man looking for an HR job, I drove into Ford

Dagenham in my Mini – not wise and very naïve.

You might get a variant on this question concerning the prospective firm's latest advertising campaign, so be prepared.

26. How is your health?

This is a killer if you have suffered from ill health. Remember, although you must not lie, nor do you have to tell the whole truth and providing you are fit enough to do the job on offer you can try a fudge answer. Unless you are unlucky enough to have a professional grilling you, you will probably get off the hook.

For example:

> **Well, my health like everyone's goes up and down, but I am pleased to say that I am really fit. Health is important to me so I usually get to the gym two or three times a week.**

The fact that you are going to the gym to strengthen your heart and bring down your blood pressure is neither here nor there, providing you are reasonably fit at this moment in time.

A professional will ask 'How many days off work did you have through sickness in the last 12 months?' and 'When was the last time you had five continuous days or more away from work due to illness?'

Direct questions require direct answers but even here you can soften the impact:

> **On the xxx project last year I was working 16-hour days and I really had to fight for resources, so it is little wonder that one week following its successful completion, my body took its revenge. I am pleased to say that I am very fit now. Health is important to**

me so I usually get to the gym two or three times a
week.

Even here you are not saying your minor heart attack
took you out for three months. However, it is critical
that you do not take on a position which will adversely
affect your health, just as it would be unfair of an
employer to take you on if the company was sick and
knew your job was up for retrenchment.

27. What has taken your interest in the news recently?
Nothing to do with the job and all to do with how well
informed or well rounded you are. At one time it was a
standard question for graduates and school leavers
which has somehow spilt over into general interviewing.
At best your answer could give an indication of your
comprehension, analytical and communication skills.
The advice here is to read an editorial in the *Economist*
that week just in case you get this sort of question.

Good manners

There is no such thing as the perfect interview. Even if you have answered all the questions perfectly, on the way home, as you reflect on the questions you were asked, there will be that awful moment when you realise what you could have said and what you left out. That is the bad news. The good news is that having thought about the drift of the questions and their themes, you will have a much better idea of what the company is looking for and the ideal candidate.

Now strike while the iron is hot and write back to the interviewer with a thank you letter – the subtext of the communication is to give him or her additional reasons for hiring you.

The thank you letter also has several additional advantages including:

- It shows good manners
- It displays your written communication skills
- It reminds the employer of your name
- It shows that you are motivated
- It shows that you are very interested in the job

but above all:

It gives additional reasons for giving you the job.

Several times, in my experience, the employer has made the offer to a better candidate only to find that applicant has been snapped up by another employer. This being the case who do you think will come to mind as the preferred second choice? No doubt that would be the one who has given additional reasons as to why they should be hired.

What to say? Try something along these lines:

Dear Mr Hutton
May I say how much I enjoyed our meeting last Thursday when we discussed my application for the position of Logistics Manager at your Liverpool facility.

On reflection it might be useful for you to know that I also have skills and experience in xxx where I achieved xxx for the company.

Obviously I am writing to you because I am most interested in the position and I am confident that I can make an immediate contribution in the role.

Once again, thank you for your time and I look forward to hearing from you.

Yours sincerely,

Of course – as in life so in job search – there are no guarantees, but a letter such as the above is not going to harm your chances and may just tip the balance in your favour.

Some have objected to the follow-up letter saying that it is too much of a 'suck up' or a sign of desperation. Our experience in consultancy is that you should never be too keen to want a job. If you were an employer and you had two candidates who could do the job equally well, but one gave that little extra, which one would you go for – the aloof or the keen? 'Treat them mean and keep them keen' applies to other areas of life, and even there it is doubtful.

Doing due diligence on the job

Just because you have been offered the job does not mean that you should take it without doing some due diligence on the position. Job and career choice would be another book (in fact it is called the *Perfect Career* and is a sister book to this) but here are some questions you would do well to discover before you sign the contract.

Many of these questions you can ask once you have had the job offer. Ask them before and it is a safe bet that you are causing too much aggravation and the offer will go elsewhere. At a senior level you are given an opportunity to visit the organisation and meet your future colleagues and talk with your team of subordinates. Then is the time to drill down on these points before you commit your career and your future to this company. Remember, just as the company has chosen you, so too should you be choosing it. Careers should be a two-way motorway not a one-way street.

ABOUT THE JOB

- Why or how has the job become vacant? If you are going to fill the shoes of someone else, what

happened to the previous incumbent and why?
- What are the specific short- and medium-term KPIs?
- How and when is your performance reviewed and by whom?
- What are the major challenges in the job in the foreseeable future?
- Is the nature of the job likely to alter in terms of technology/market/organisational changes in the foreseeable future?
- What resources, both technical and human, go with the position?
- Who are the other members of your team and the teams you will have working for you?

ABOUT CAREER PROSPECTS

- How does this job fit into your career and life plan?
- What is the reasonable tenure for this job?
- What will be your next job after this position? Will it be within or outside this company?
- How will this job develop your skills and competencies?
- What are the chances for training/courses/professional development?

ABOUT THE COMPANY

- Is the company growing, shrinking or static?
- What is the reputation of the company within its sector?
- Has the company ever been a target for a takeover or been in merger talks?

- Has the company ever downsized and how did it treat those who were retrenched?
- Is the company unionised and will you be expected to join?

Questions you should ask yourself before accepting an offer

Everyone is entitled to make at least one career mistake but, like sports injuries, the older you are, the more difficult it is to recover. Unless you really must, the advice is do not take a job unless, for financial reasons, you really have to. When you get your first job offer rejoice and be glad because the market place, which is always choosy, is telling you some very positive things about you and your job search including:

- You are marketing yourself correctly
- Your CV is working and achieving interviews
- Your interview skills are first class
- The market place is prepared to buy you

All this should convince you that if you can get one job offer you can get another. So now is the time to think through some of the following questions to ensure that you are making the right career choice. We use Hertzberg's hygiene/motivation classification for convenience.

HYGIENE QUESTIONS

- Can I do the job?
- Am I fit enough to do the job?
- Are the logistic requirements acceptable to me and my family (location, travel to work time, work travel and periods away, etc.)?
- Does the salary match the going market rate, my expectations and is it realistic for my commitments both now and for the foreseeable future?
- Are the hours (contractual and expected) acceptable to my lifestyle so I can work to live and not live to work?
- Can I get to and from work easily and not get stressed through the journey?
- Is my work environment comfortable and does it meet my status needs?
- Is my work environment safe?
- Is there reasonable job security?

MOTIVATIONAL QUESTIONS

- Does the organisational value system match my own?
- Can I get passionate about what I have to do and what is expected of me?
- Can I relate to and be in harmony with the product/service or organisation? (Some people have ethical difficulties such as working in Defence or tobacco products.)
- Does this job improve my long-term employability?
- Will the experience from this job position me well for my next career move?
- Are the career prospects good and realistic?

- Will I work well with my manager?
- Will I enjoy working with the team?
- Will I get the support and resources I need to be successful?

Don't get the job offer?

If there is a better candidate than you, it does not matter how perfect your answers are, you will not get the offer. Is this bad news? No. When you get close to a job offer the market place is telling you that your skills and experience are purchasable and that it is only a question of time and a few more applications before you get bought. Even the best salesperson knows that he has to make several presentations before a sale is made, but the fact that he is making presentations at all convinces him that the market place wants what he or she has to offer and so it is a question of time.

Even if you don't get the job there is still an advantage for you in that the interview is a learning opportunity. It is obvious and hardly needs saying that the more interviews you go to, the better you will get at them.

If you suffer interview anxiety, every interview you attend will help you overcome your emotional stress. Remember when you first went abroad and worried during the trip about customs and where to collect your luggage? Once you have been abroad a few times, you find yourself enjoying the trip rather than worrying. Interviews are the same: you will find yourself enjoying the process, confident that for every interview you have you are that much closer to a job offer.

Remember to ask yourself the following questions:

- How did it go?
- What went well?
- What did not go well?
- What was difficult?
- What did I learn?
- What further research must I do?
- How can I follow up?

About the author

Max A. Eggert is Chief Psychologist with Transcareer, a consultancy that is dedicated to assisting individuals to achieve their career dreams.

Other books by Max in this series are:

Perfect CV
Perfect Interview
Perfect Career
The Best Job Hunt Book In The World

Max first graduated in Theology before transferring his allegiance to Psychology, which was then followed by a Masters in Industrial Relations and more recently in postgraduate work in Clinical Hypnosis.

When not writing, coaching or running seminars, Max has two other passions: riding his thoroughbreds and dancing Ceroc. As an Anglican priest he is an active member of the parish team at St Mary the Virgin in Waverley NSW.

Should you wish to be coached by Max, have him provide a workshop, speak at a conference or move your career forward by working with one of the highly experienced Transcareer Team in the UK or Australia then please just email him at max@transcareer.com.au

Remember

'How you approach the interview will be taken as the way you approach the job.'

'It is not the best person that gets the job but the one that is best on the day of the interview.'

'Be successful'.

Max A. Eggert
Bondi Beach
NSW, Australia